70 Days of Reign

An Inner Guide to Transform Your Life

Kristie Kennedy

Acknowledgments

After years of working in toxic environments, I chose to re-define success, re-design my life and re-align my personal values. The new Kristie is void of workaholism which once contributed to a lack of self-care. She is lavishly robed in regal garments of life, love, liberty, and laughter.

I honor my loving husband Lamont Ward, who inspires me daily to step outside of my comfort zone. I am grateful for a man who watches over me daily, affirms my purpose, challenges my potential, believes in my dreams, and blankets me with serenity and tranquility. His strong and gentle arms are more than I dared to hope for. God saw fit to send me a noble knight—gentle and understanding. His tenderness keeps me grounded; his divine essence leaves me astounded. Cultured, creative and charismatic. In my eyes, chivalry is far from gone, this love is always right and never wrong. Excellence is what you get when you refuse to settle for less than heaven's best. Every day of my life is a grand celebration. I am blessed to be covered, protected and esteemed without limitations. The priceless gems housed in my soul remain untold, for I've discovered true wealth and riches that a million banks could never hold. A soul mate is the most priceless gift anyone can ever be blessed with. Thank you, many times, over for being my soul mate. My world is reassured by you, my tomorrows need to have you near, so many of my smiles depend on you, and my heart is thankful that you're forever mine. This is not a fairy tale... my dream life is real, and I am no longer waiting to exhale.

I cherish my faithful mother Annie Kennedy who has believed in every wild and crazy dream I've ever dreamed. I celebrate the memory of my passionate father who taught me how to fight for a future greater than the pain of my past. A special thank you to my closest covenant friends for your constant love, prayers, and support.

To every reader, you are the reason I rose early in the morning and stayed up late at night. I only want to see you reign in your divine domain. I celebrate your personal transformation that will transpire from every word breathed. To God be the glory for the grace to create *HIS*tory and the strength to pursue my destiny with relentless tenacity.

Queenfidence Dedication

In loving memory of my first speaking agent and precious friend, Joanna R. Finney who slipped away from earth's grasp on January 1, 2018, at the ripe age of thirty-one. She believed wholeheartedly in the vision of Queenfidence and worked untiringly to promote its message. Her example of passionate living inspires me to mark the moments daily and make every single one count for all eternity. "This is our year."

Foreword

Prescribed to each of us, it seems, are a set of missteps, upsets, and regrets throughout life. They are never more than we can bear, rather they are just enough to make us quite uncomfortable with being comfortable. In these seasons, we are stretched beyond our mental, emotional, and spiritual capacity and an open invitation to reign in our Queenfidence is extended for each of us to embrace.

If you desire to be inspired and empowered through your stretching season, you have picked up the right book. In Queenfidence: 70 Days of Reign, Kristie Kennedy pours out of her experiences as a life coach, image consultant, and spiritual advisor to escort you to your throne of breakthrough. Whether you've been timid in your career, and you know it's beyond time for a promotion; or you're tired of settling in relationships, yet you're challenged by the fear of being alone; or you've been your own roadblock to success as you battle imposter syndrome and self-sabotage—allow the Kan Do Koach to teach you how to straighten your crown and reign in your divine domain.

I am confident that daily dedication to the readings and activities in this book will train you to take authority over your life. I speak from personal experience, as Kristie's coaching over the years has shifted my mindset, my self-worth, and my faith journey. I've also witnessed her words bless CEO's, entrepreneurs, principals, healthcare professionals, and thousands more at national and regional conferences, such as her Elevate to Great VIP coaching sessions and

Temple Fit Co.'s annual women's wellness conference.

Skilled psalmist and poet, Kristie had you on her heart as she penned and prayed over each word of this book. Queen with big dreams, get ready to dust off your robe and polish your crown, because it's time to shine.

Dr. Asha

"Creator of Healthy Conversations"

Author of Eat, *Drink, Do: 3 Basic Principles for Health by the Bible*

Introduction

It is no coincidence that I am standing on the threshold of divine prominence. I've crawled through the ashes of adversity and laid barren in a desert of defeat. Yet, like a star in the night, I chose to rise high above my dismal plight. Every day I took one step forward with the eyes of a tiger, the heart of a lion, the speed of a cheetah, the poise of a panther and with a crown of fire. I created my own champion shift anthem. **No-one is you, and that is your power.** I leaned into my faith and decided to turn a pink slip into Queenfidence.

I am intentionally here to release words of affirmation into your inner being. Despite challenges, your spirit is greater than the cocoon that has held you captive. Prepare to spread your wings and dare to dream bigger dreams. The power of momentum is driven by your ability to not only see but to act on what you believe.

Early one morning, I was sifting through a folder with collected stories and stumbled across this simple yet powerful message. In old wars, an English drummer boy was taken prisoner by the French. They amused themselves by making the lad play on his instrument and asked him to sound the retreat. The drummer boy answered proudly, "I have never learned how to play that sound." I encourage you to give voice to victory and never a victim mentality.

We each have the power to rise from an ocean of despair and defeat every opponent that contests our call to greatness. To become all that you are destined to be will require an unwavering obstinacy.

Pursuing your purpose with passion is a lifelong endeavor. Countless individuals are often derailed from the path of success as a result of their preoccupation with critics, adversity, and disappointments. It is 100% possible to be triumphant in trouble and victorious in the vacillating valleys of life.

My Purpose

As a women's empowerment speaker who provides confidence and clarity coaching to female leaders and business executives, my purpose is to deliver the keys to limitless possibilities. I ignite dormant passion and infuse them with the bold belief that they can conquer any obstacle standing in their way. My purpose is to awaken the woman who has been sleeping on her greatness and reaffirm her worth by inspiring her to realize that any pain she has encountered was a divine invitation to rule and reign. My purpose is to be a river of refreshing for the exhausted woman who is tired of playing small and being the world's best-kept secret. My purpose is to provoke the fearful woman who is ready to claim center stage as the star of her own life, powerfully shift in mind and dare to magnificently rise to unprecedented heights.

What is significant about the number seventy? It reflects perfect spiritual order and restoration of all things in my life. Before I married my husband, my first, middle and last name all had seven letters. This discovery was significantly validating to me especially after years of battling low self-esteem. It was the catalyst to embracing the truth that I was created whole, with nothing missing or broken. I began to re-define myself from the inside out and re-design my life one bold action step at a time. As your inner guide, I am honored to walk with you through the valley low until you rise beyond the mountain high. We each must decide to take our rightful place in leadership if we plan to leave a lasting mark that cannot be erased.

The Power to Start

A girl with dreams ultimately becomes a woman with a vision, and every vision will take a village of selfless support. I am reminded of my sixth-grade teacher who handed me a journal that forever impacted my life. My high school counselor who advocated for me attending college. My business mentor who enlightened me on the power of entrepreneurship. My close friend who told me to never allow money to dictate what I could or could not do, and my selfless mother who worked two and three jobs to pay for higher education. In appreciation of all who have empowered me to become more than I could ever perceive, I have dedicated my brilliance to igniting hearts, inspiring minds, and impacting lives.

After over twenty years of self-discovery, daunting disappointments, delightful adventures, and personal dream fulfillment, I have accumulated a wealth of knowledge to share with emerging voices who are courageously stepping in the aura of their own light.

According to Chinese philosophy, "The journey of a thousand miles begins with a single step." In other words, **even the longest journey must begin from where you stand**. For many dreamers, this first step seems to be the most painstaking, yet it is the most vital of all. You need a great heart to start and even greater resolve to not cease moving your feet. This bold step into the unknown appears to be the main barrier of one's progress towards personal achievement. The underlying apprehension rests in the thought that a massive undertaking could not possibly be accomplished by our own hands. When you embody an unwavering faith in limitless possibilities, there is no obstacle too high or barrier too low to prevent you from achieving your goals. The power of momentum rests in the fuel to move forward despite paralyzing fears, insecurities, self-sabotaging beliefs, excuses, limited resources which include lack of time, start-up funds, knowledge, experience, and human capital.

The Courage to Stand

As I planned to exit corporate America and focus on my first launch into entrepreneurship full-time over twenty years ago, I expressed these intimate thoughts on leadership.

Tonight, I went shopping for décor to put in the building. If I have to go at it alone for a season, I am willing to give my all. It's been over a month and two weeks since I signed the lease for my business. I have been preparing mentally for the transition. I just checked out ten books on leadership. I really want to be the best leader that I can be. I don't focus on the fact that I've never been an upfront leader. I am willing to learn how to demonstrate exactly what I desire others to emulate.

As you begin to courageously pursue your deepest dreams, there may only be a handful of supporters. In actuality, that is a fair amount due to the extensive hours you will be logging in just to make a print in the sands of time.

The Fears to Conquer

Recently, I was asked, "How do you overcome fear?" We must first define fear. If you can clearly perceive an emotion, you can identify it upon its arrival in your mind. Fear always speaks behind the prison bars of falsehood. The only way you conquer fear is with truth. It is perfectly normal to experience this fleeting and negative emotion. We must move through fear with bold confidence if we expect to behold our loftiest aspirations. In the silence of my own struggle to keep treading forward, I noted, *I am taking it moment by moment. Sometimes I ask myself did I make the right decision? Did I step out too fast? Should I have saved up more money? A multitude of thoughts bombarded my mind. Yet, if I didn't take the leap into a life of limitlessness, I would be asking myself, should I leave this job? Why am I still here? Should I work part-time? Wherever we are in life, human nature demands questions and answers.*

The Passion to Persevere

In the words of Benjamin Franklin, "The things which hurt, instruct." I will never forget the pain of watching my dream dissipate before my very eyes. There was no explanation that could bring immediate comfort during the pinnacle of my emotional tidal wave. After being in a new building for two months, I closed the doors due to a financial deficit that stemmed from the lack of sales, marketing, and planning, etc. Launching out into the deep waters of entrepreneurship is risky business, and it is the main reason individuals never stretch themselves beyond what their natural eyes can see. As I glance over the chronicles of yesterday, my heart is filled with joy knowing I survived the seemingly insurmountable pain of hardship. Initially, my focus was in the wrong place as I was determined to build a business when all along the business was building an unshakeable leader inside of me. If you are afraid to make mistakes, you are simply not ready to learn and evolve into a person of influence. It doesn't matter how many times you fall flat on your face when you remain unswerving in your convictions; it will lift you from the pit of failure into stellar heights of success.

The Discipline to Focus

During the extended financial famine and after losing the building, I became extremely clouded in judgment. Honestly, I don't know how I garnered the strength to keep going while financially hemorrhaging. On one particular day, I took advantage of a complimentary business coaching session from a married couple. The sound advice they gave me provided death shattering light. My challenge was to focus on what it was I truly wanted to do and assess my natural strengths. As they spoke into my future and urged me to get crystal clear saying, "Until you gain clarity you will not be able to compel others to partner in your vision." Lastly, they emphatically asserted, **"The confused mind always says no."** In this busy world, we live in clarity is often difficult to achieve because it is born from a deep place overshadowed by stillness. Countless entrepreneurs fall into the snares of distraction at the hands of shiny new opportunities. Those who innovate and thrive on a consistent basis have harnessed the discipline of focus.

The Rewards of Labor

The call of entrepreneurship requires selfless service to the public and an undeniable sacrifice of time. On days when I feel as though I have nothing left to give, out of the blue someone shares with me how my life has touched them in a significant way. At that moment I am gently reminded every teardrop and bead of sweat is worth the effort. One night, I began to jot unedited thoughts, *'Wow, this has been some weekend. I have been working non-stop. I didn't know I could work so hard. I don't have a lot of help but the help that I do have is good help from people who love me dearly.'* When I sat in a workshop on entrepreneurship, my desire was to make loads of money and have the freedom to enjoy it. I never knew the extent of the work involved behind the scenes. To put things in perspective, imagine working five jobs at once. As you delve into the ever-changing seas of entrepreneurship, remember we were not created to watch from the mainland and "a smooth sea never made a skillful sailor." Despise not the day of small beginnings as you create a massive track record of continuous winning.

I am who I am
created in the image and likeness of God-that's truth
I am not what I do
with a hidden aspiration to collect brownie points

for a job well done disseminated by you

I am authentic

call me eccentric

I prefer intrinsically artistic

I am un-phased by such an illegitimate assessment

of what you perceive I have been predestined to be

I am the one who has survived unyielding despair in

soul barren trenches gasping and reaching for breath

after my strength dissipated into thin air

I am a force of determination,

a pillow of meekness often viewed as weakness

yet I stand in peace on a plateau of greatness

I am the fuel burning in a flame of fire

at the end of a recital

a single note remembered,

the key change most talked about- simply undeniable

I am the teacher who appears to the student seeking to be freed

of their deepest fears

I am the woman who would not, could not, dare not throw in the

towel when my spirit sank beneath the ground, in the face of the

storm I kissed it

In a game of chess hailed as the queen, never a pawn, I am relentless

I am who I am, dislike me if you must- for I was created in the image

of God

and I choose to shadow His reflection from dawn until dusk

I am who I am, not who I was nor all that I shall be

wholly, completely, authentically

I accept and love myself unconditionally

Now the question is, can you handle the real "Me"?

Table of Contents

Perfectionism

The setting of unrealistic and demanding goals accompanied by a disposition to regard failure to achieve them as unacceptable and a sign of personal worthlessness.

Dear Queen,

How long will you convince yourself that what you've settled for is what you've secretly savored? I once heard a woman say, "I have been writing a book for over thirteen years because the content doesn't seem to be good enough." What goal are you putting off due to feelings of inadequacy? How many reasons are you clinging to as authentic justifications? Do you feel as if you are unqualified to be a leading voice for your generation?

Consider all that which procrastination and perfectionism are robbing you of:

- Time freedom
- Greater joy
- Increased wealth
- Influence
- Peace of mind
- Opportunities
- Strategic partnerships

The list is inexhaustible. It's easy to verbalize all that we find dissatisfying in our lives, yet it requires purposeful intention to let go of unproductive thought and behavioral patterns. Every day is filled with brand-new opportunities to celebrate internal progress. Do not fall into the trap of perfectionism; it will only stunt your growth and diminish your brilliance. Take time throughout the day to listen to your own heartbeat. Does it beat fast, slow or medium tempo? Release what needs to go and embrace what is welcome to flow. Be willing to search for calm in the cave of chaos, peace in the plight of pressure and resolve in the rampage of resistance.

In the words of Anatole France, "To accomplish great things we must not only act but also dream; not only plan but also believe."

There is a unique time-stamped opportunity to change our world for the better and influence bright minds ripe with untapped potential. Nora Ephron powerfully stated, "Above all, be the heroine of your life and not the victim." **How will you rise above uncertainty with the flame of victory resting in the palm of your hands?** Discontentment and disillusionment are buried in the bosom of the one seeking a perfect path to destiny, prosperity, and freedom. The broken road you stand upon can be a spectacular springboard catapulting you into adventures never known. This could be the finest hour of your life if you dare to seize every ounce of genius hidden inside.

One of my business mentors posted a quote online that pierced my core. It read, "Don't look for inspiration, inspire." Will you dare to play by the rules you write? Can you envision yourself being the director of your own life story? Are you willing to sacrifice comfort in exchange for conquest? If tomorrow never comes, can you lift your head with pride and say, "I made the most of every second on this day? I dared to seize my dreams, unapologetically."

If we are honest, it all boils down to one single word: excuses. An insightful definition of excuses coined by an unknown author, described them as "tools of incompetence, used to build monuments of nothingness, and those who specialize in them seldom accomplish anything."

Many people kill the wrong thing. Strive to execute (plan) your expectancies and execute (kill) your excuses. Contrary to popular belief, the easiest thing to do is start, and the hardest thing to do is quit. If you have been inactive for an extended period of time, taking even the first step forward can seem intimidating. We often talk ourselves out of success and into failure due to the misconception that it appears out of reach.

There are three types of self-sabotaging mindsets that you must shift if you desire to excel beyond your current state of existence:

1) **Under-thinking:** A mindset characterized by low terrain acuity in which you underestimate your ability to achieve that which you set out to apprehend.

2) **Over-thinking:** A faulty perception that questions, doubts and overanalyzes what is attainable despite past failures and societal labels.

3) **Negative thinking:** A negative and pessimistic view that perceives the world through the lens of defeat rather than a telescope of triumph.

How long do you intend to sit on the sidelines of life? Where is the excitement in watching and waiting for your own unique opportunity to shine? The moment you decide to take massive action you are guaranteed to produce massive results. I know you've probably heard this statement replay in your mind over a million times. "I could do that if given the chance." **You possess the capability to create a beautiful legacy.**

When you begin to recognize your innate value, the world will stand at attention and take notice. Grant yourself the green light and go after what you knowingly deserve. Rummaging for an endorsement to walk in the power of your purpose will leave you deflated and discouraged.

Ralph Waldo Emerson profoundly stated, "Do that which you are afraid to do, and the death of fear is certain." Soaring boldly to unfathomable heights requires a winning mentality and the audacity to defy all odds stacked against you.

How do you shatter the stained glassed windows of perfectionism and courageously embrace a brand-new day of change? As simple as this: decide to be and do something dangerously different. Take heed to the wisdom of Johann Wolfgang von Goethe. "What is not started today is never finished tomorrow." It is vital to understand that ideas without implementation are merely good intentions, which rarely inspire individuals to ascend to the pinnacles of prosperity.

Grant yourself the gift of grace and remember, "Progress is perfection." Celebrate every imperfect step you've had the guts to take. The truth is, we never know what we're capable of until we are challenged. In a purpose defining moment we either rise to the occasion or remain hidden in the corridors of complacency.

You are a rare gift to a society that needs more sparkle. Are you excited for another chance to enhance your luminosity and glow your own way? Choreographer Martha Graham boldly declared, "Nobody cares if you can't dance well. Just get up and dance. Great dancers are not great because of their technique. They are great because of their passion."

Finally, I challenge you to accomplish the sacred work you were placed on earth to complete. In the soul-stirring words of Jennifer King Lindley, "Let go of the drive to do everything perfectly and let go of the self-recrimination that comes when you don't. It's the quickest way to becoming truly content and reaching your full potential."

The greater your self-efficacy (belief), the less likely you are to disbelieve in your ability to achieve. In bone crushing adversity you can awaken grace in the face of gratitude as you dare to turn anguish into awareness and awareness into apprehension and apprehension into ascension.

On the days where you find your confidence faltering, remember The Little Engine that Could. A little railroad engine was employed about a station yard for such work as it was built for, pulling cars on and off the switches. One morning it was waiting for the next call when a long

5

train of freight-cars asked a large engine in the roundhouse to take it over the hill. "I can't; that is too much a pull for me," said the great engine built for hard work. Then the train asked another engine, and another, only to hear excuses and more refusals. In desperation, the train asked the little switch engine to draw it up the grade and down on the other side. "I think I can," puffed the little locomotive, and put itself in front of the great heavy train. As it went on the little engine kept bravely puffing faster and faster, "I think I can, I think I can, I think I can." As it neared the top of the grade, which had so discouraged the larger engines, it went slowed. However, it kept saying, "I—think—I—can, I—think—I—can." It reached the top by drawing on bravery and then went on down the grade, congratulating itself by saying, "I thought I could, I thought I could."

Will you be as daring as the little engine and demonstrate what is possible when you think profoundly, speak passionately and lead powerfully?

C.P.I.L.L. Confidence Prescription for Progress

Crownfirmation: I am omnificent, capable of creating and accomplishing anything. I walk in omnidirectional focus, favor, freedom, and fortune.

Pause to Ponder: What perfectionist thoughts are holding you back from springing forward? If you were to take a moment to sit alone in silence and hear the faintest whisper, what would your heart ask you to do? Where does it desire to lead you? Can you imagine how many rewards are in store if you choose to follow and leave behind every trace of inhibition lingering inside? Why do you cling so tightly to a life that is less than you quietly imagine it could possibly be? Get to the root of this issue.

I Celebrate:

Leadership Lesson Learned:

Lifestyle Elevation: Every Day I Will,

Wholeness

To be physically sound and emotionally healthy, free of disease or deformity, wound or injury.

Dear Queen,

I experienced incredible amounts of pain throughout my young adult years, often attributable to self-imposed decisions. It took decades to facilitate colossal healing and learn how to become my own emotional wellness advocate. I realized that until I expected more of myself and others, I would continue to attract toxic individuals into the salubrious space I carefully constructed. My mantra was, **"What I permit, will persist."** As I stand unbroken on the other side of heartache, it is a beautiful haven of rest that my spirit delights to dwell in. I believe whole people are empowered to heal wounded people who are lost in a chasm of confusion.

Have you ever felt overlooked, cast aside and invisible to your environmental surroundings? Are you worn out from the internal fight and just wanting to get your life back on track? Has nerve-wracking pain left you numb? Do you crave more? You are not alone. Maybe you are experiencing the cold winds of alienation right now. The question that must be posed is, "Why am I seeking the stamp of approval from others who are completely disconnected from me as an individual?"

We often feel undervalued because we believe others are obligated to embrace our plight, our past, our purpose for being. We allow unhealthy thoughts of feeling underappreciated, overlooked and overworked to become the impetus of an emotional breakdown. It is imperative during these tender moments when you experience a dip in your confidence to remind yourself who you are, why you're here, and what you see when you look in the mirror.

If this feeling of anonymity is still lingering from past experiences, it may be time to examine how you can re-invent a more powerful version of yourself. Can you visualize a bold, brilliant and beautiful woman too amazing to blend in the background of any crowd?

The demands of our responsibilities can leave us depleted and emotionally defeated. Are you feeling overwhelmed with internal frustrations? Does it appear as if everyone getting the best pieces of you and you're exhausted from running on empty fumes? When you finally catch your breath at the end of the day, you are left scurrying for mere crumbs to feast upon. **As a result of being overachievers, we secretly nurse in silence wounds of weariness, which remain long after an exceptional performance is done.** I am here to release you from people-pleasing tendencies and suffocating unhealthy habits. Listen, you have the power and the right to say no to anything that fails to affirm your self-worth.

Honor the sanity of your mind by refusing to be continuously overextended in work, life, and service. The body is designed to heal and restore itself. I challenge you to pause in sweet serenity throughout the week with less stress and enjoy the sweet nectar of divine rest. There is nothing honorable in neglecting yourself because you want to appear without flaw, masquerading as an impenetrable force to be reckoned with.

In all honesty, we are the only ones responsible for our successes and failures. You can keep your emotional tank overflowing with peace and joy when you begin to cultivate a garden of self-love. Develop a strong sense of appreciation for the unique woman that you are and the style in which you showcase dignity in a dungeon of despair.

As you come to terms with the liberating notion of being perfectly whole and fully accepted apart from anyone's validation, a new-found freedom to be your most authentic-self will unfold.

You have the power to live life on a larger stage than you are currently standing on. As you take full ownership of your rare qualities, the masses will recognize what an extraordinary treasure you are.

Trust your voice. Listen to the whisper that says you deserve more. Don't ignore the red flags. There is a blossoming rose waiting for your hands to hold an inch below your nose. Give yourself the gift of wholeness.

If you are ready to stop the back and forth:

Declare to yourself, "Enough is enough."

Yes, there is immeasurably more to embrace, expand and explore.

Remember, this is your life.

Re-write the script and make sure your best-selling story of elevation produces a standing ovation.

In the words of Tony Robbins, "By changing nothing, nothing changes." How will you treat life differently from this instant in order to move forward? The power to change is embedded in the will to refocus in an alternate direction charting an audacious new course.

C.P.I.L.L. Confidence Prescription for Progress

Crownfirmation: I trust the still small voice inside of my heart to safely lead me to a refreshing well of worthiness and wholeness.

Pause to Ponder: What do you desire to richly experience in life, love, and liberty at this very second?

I Celebrate:

Leadership Lesson Learned:

Lifestyle Elevation: Every Day I Will,

Day 3

Evolve

To make visible or manifest, to produce especially by deliberate effort over time, to unfold gradually and expand by a process of growth.

Dear Queen,

Who you are and where you are right now is a mere reflection of the life experiences cradled in your heart. How often do you express the desire for bigger and better opportunities to come your way? If opportunity were to knock on your door at this very hour can you honestly say you are ready to answer with a reverberating yes?

It is easy to miss the unseen value in waiting for the opportune moment of desired longings to arrive. In our anxiety to clutch what is next, we fail to cultivate the necessary skills and character to walk admirably towards the most premium possibilities available to us.

Do you seek to tread on a higher playing field and soar into greater dimensions of influence? Of course you do, but fear has kept you on a tight leash. The power to break free is just one deep breath away locked inside the bellows of your faith. The key to your liberty lies in the words you unleash into any stifling environment. In order to speak powerfully, you must think profoundly. Examine every square inch of any belief that makes you shrink. As the sun rises and falls, commit to becoming a vigilant watch guard over the inner gates of your mindset.

The path towards destiny is filled with bountiful lessons to be harnessed. Underneath the hardships you've encountered, wisdom will peer through the shadows of uncertainty providing a vivid light for the destination ahead. There is no need to rush wildly into greatness, as it is written everything under heaven has a perfect season to be unveiled. Believe wholeheartedly, that all things will work together for your favor and good.

As you advance forward remember these three keys to succeed:

1) **What you allow will continue.** If you never challenge your employer for a raise, it may never be actualized. If you never charge what you're worth in business, you may never receive it. Listen, if they have the audacity to ask for a service, you must have a greater one to expect full compensation. You are free to extract your brilliance from anyone who does not value your presence.

2) **Serve your excuses an eviction notice.** Be willing to sift through the manure in order to enjoy the magnificent. As a faithful steward over your time, do not forget that no is a powerful and complete sentence.

3) **Success is not a place.** Success is a mental posture that expands daily. Transformational leaders ascend from within and win. The best thoughts lead to the best choices which create the best outcomes that ultimately produce the best life.

In the words of Henry David Thoreau, "Go confidently in the direction of your dreams. Live the life you've always imagined." Though impossible it may seem and quite out of reach, one day you and your heart's desire will finally meet. Intense resolve is required to evolve. Are you prepared for promotion or simply going through the motions? To do so, you must:

- Expand your mindset. Nothing massive occurs by being passive.

- Vision your way there. See it, say it, seize it and soar.

- Overcome adversity with optimism and boldly believe.

- Lead by example and invite the hungry to eat with you.

- Venture into new territories and excavate untapped potential.

- Empty yourself of all negative energy and create space to be occupied by victory, not defeat.

"May your dreams be larger than mountains and may you have the courage to scale their summits."

–Harley King

C.P.I.L.L. Confidence Prescription for Progress

Crownfirmation: I refuse to allow fear to control my mind, my body or my life as I manifest my deepest desires.

Pause to Ponder: What fears surround the thought of evolving into who you envision your next best self to be?

I Celebrate:

Leadership Lesson Learned:

Lifestyle Elevation: Every Day I Will,

Worthy

Having sufficient worth, value or importance.

Dear Queen,

Oliver Burkeman wrote a simple yet profound short story that captures the power of owning your worth called, *A Turn of the Screw*. There was an industrialist whose production line inexplicably breaks down, costing him millions of dollars per day. He finally tracks down an expert who takes out a screwdriver, turns one screw and then as the factory cranks back up to life, he presents a bill for $10,000. Affronted, the factory owner demands an itemized version. The expert is happy to oblige. For turning a screw: $1.00. For knowing which screw to turn: $9,999.00.

Are you struggling with recognizing your self-worth and boldly reinforcing to others your personal value? I remember writing my first book, *Upon the Tables of My Heart*, a collection of poetic prose. The introspective questions I began to ask myself were:

1) Who am I to love myself?

2) Who am I to have big dreams?

3) Who am I to believe I could do anything?

4) Who am I to think that I am someone special?

5) Who am I to accept all that God created me to be?

6) Who am I when others refuse to accept me as I am?

7) Who am I?

8) Who am I not to know who I am?

After experiencing one failed relationship after another, my perceived self-value began to plummet. It was paramount that I quiet every outside voice and listen within to hear my own opinions. We may never verbally articulate that we don't feel worthy of the best life has to offer, yet our internal disposition is often reflected through our actions. It is clearly expressed by the position we take in relationships, our posture in the workplace, and how we nurture our physical bodies on a daily basis.

I know it may be hard to breathe right now, hard to believe right now, and hard to break free right now.

First, it is important that you identify why you feel unworthy. Is there a specific incident that you encountered recently or a painful and unresolved situation from your past that needs to be addressed? It is undoubtedly an impossible feat to conquer what you refuse to confront. If the wound is too deep a burden to bear alone, consider a trusted friend or counselor to initiate the process of healing. This is one of the most vital steps because if the foundation is faulty, the house will collapse when the storms of life begin to rage.

Secondly, you are now equipped to empower others with the insight you have gained on your voyage of self-discovery. It is easy to discount all the challenges you've overcome and say, "I just did what I had to do." The distinctive perspective you possess is priceless, especially for someone who is encountering a similar situation seeking answers. They need someone who can empathize, synthesize and help actualize a solution to their problem.

Thirdly, broadcast your brilliance everywhere you go. You must dare to shout it from the rooftops until the whole world knows you hold the secret key to breaking free. The very definition of brilliance is intense brightness of light. Yes, you will be tempted to crawl back into the shell of obscurity, but you will be rudely awakened when you discover that you no longer fit. You'll have outgrown the hollow trenches of insignificance that sheltered your insecurities, fears, and inadequacies.

When it's the fight of your life, you want a miracle in your corner. Trust what your heart believes more than what your natural eyes can see. Step into a spacious land of limitlessness where abundance dwells bountifully.

Yes, it's real. Yes, it's where you belong. Yes, you deserve it. Yes, you can have more. Yes, you are worthy. Yes, you are loved. Yes, you are whole. Yes, you are stronger than ever before. Yes, you have the power to let go. Yes, you can walk in liberty. Yes, you are unfastened from the chains of scarcity. Yes, to success and nothing less than God's best. Yes, life is bliss and you were born for such a time as this.

Woman of worth

I celebrate you.

for rising from the ashes of your past

The sorrow of your situation and

the barriers set against you.

I celebrate you for the battles you've won

accompanied by your kind and generous heart.

I celebrate your calm, cool resolve

and your hard-earned determination to overcome.

I celebrate your dreams, your vision, your future

your fortitude and your destiny.

I celebrate your soft femininity and fierce faith.

I celebrate your good works and brilliant mind.

Woman of worth, beautiful and magnificent

Shine *big* and burn *bright.*

C.P.I.L.L. Confidence Prescription for Progress

Crownfirmation: I grant myself permission to extract my greatness from every environment that refuses to embrace my presence as a priceless present.

Pause to Ponder: If you could paint a picture of your self-worth what would it look, sound, and feel like?

I Celebrate:

Leadership Lesson Learned:

Lifestyle Elevation: Every Day I Will,

Day 5

Focus

A point of concentration.

Dear Queen,

I know you're on the verge of falling apart at the seams. You've rolled the dice more than once, and you're anxiously waiting to see your number turn up. Every day you ask yourself is the risk worth the reward? Is the pain worth the price? Is sacrifice worth the success? Yes, it is.

With all the odds stacked against you, I dare you to bet on your future. You have the internal fortitude to leap over any rut. I salute the strength you stand in under the tent of turbulence. I salute your resolute and resilient spirit in the face of unflinching difficulty. I salute your diligence in the daylight of despair. I salute your colorful creativity in the chamber of chaos. I salute your tenacity to walk in truth through the most tumultuous times of testing. I salute the power to prevail over pressure and pain. I salute the blazing lighthouse of leadership you beam for all to behold.

When navigating through a cumbersome hurdle, decide to explore the issue from all angles. We often laser focus in on what we can only perceive immediately. The uncommon solution rarely makes logical sense. It is critical to re-direct your perspective away from what bothers you and engage in what brightens you. Emotions carry the potency to lift us high or weigh us down. This is why focus must be undergirded by commitment. Are you willing to be fully invested until what you expect manifests?

Whatever you focus on, you will energize. Whatever you energize, you will embody. Whatever you embody, you will empower. Whatever you empower, you will establish. Whatever you establish, you will expand. Whatever you expand, you will elevate. Use your voice, even if it shakes because the future is at stake. You must adamantly commit to doing something daring if you plan to transform into someone different.

Building a durable vision requires unwavering tenacity void of passivity. Use your vision as a compass to point towards what is coming. It is going to ache to wait. But you must wait as long as it takes, it is on the way, and it will not be late. Whenever I begin training my body through physical fitness, it requires at least four weeks of strict discipline to see a noticeable change. Discover the beauty in every moment and refuse to allow disappointments to rob you of insurmountable joy.

The storms of life have a transformative power that goes unappreciated until we see the benefit of what internal change brings. In the words of Winston Churchill, "If you're going through hell, keep going." When you exit the storm expect to be completely different than when you first entered it. An unthinkable challenge becomes a bridge way to unusual courage.

You were born with majestic wings broad enough to reach your wildest dreams. They were not created for creeping, crawling, craving or cowering. Every feather was fashioned for conquering the winds of adversity and towering over the highest mountain peak. Ralph Waldo Emerson poetically stated, "When it is dark enough, you can SEE the stars."

Unleash your focus and let it flatline your frustration. Unleash your peace and let it silence your perplexity. Unleash your strength and let it crush your sorrow. Unleash your power and let it pulverize your pain. Unleash your wisdom and let it handcuff your worries. Unleash your boldness and let it uproot your barriers. Unleash your dream and let it drown your doubts. Unleash your faith and let it free your fears. Unleash the beast until there is nothing left but victory over your internal enemies.

Move relentlessly forward and look to the left, look to the right, look down low, look up high. Look around the corner, look under the pillow, look in the tree, look to the sea. Look to the foe, look to the wind, look to the bank. Look to the bridge, look to the least likely place, look to your faith. Look to the pain, look to the promise, look to the hope, look to the light and look deep inside.

There is a vacant space in this world waiting for you to occupy and own your zone of genius. Be bold, be relentless and unapologetically take hold of your designated territory.

Keep looking, keep living, keep leading and keep learning. The future is here, the future is now, and the future is yours.

"What you seek, is seeking you."

–Rumi

C.P.I.L.L. Confidence Prescription for Progress

Crownfirmation: I am laser-focused on living with boldness in the face of iron fenced barriers.

Pause to Ponder: As you re-evaluate the activities and associations that distract you from key priorities where will you guide your energy in order to accomplish your goals expeditiously?

I Celebrate:

Leadership Lesson Learned:

Lifestyle Elevation: Every Day I Will,

Image

A visual representation of something, a picture, impression or mental conception symbolic of a basic attitude.

Dear Queen,

The culture of our nation is heavily driven by visual stimulation. Image is what others use to instinctively make an overall assessment of who you are upon an initial meeting, even if it is contrary to your core being. It is of no surprise why women spend an exorbitant amount of money each year on lotions and potions to keep their skin glowing.

Are you the type of woman who dresses casually for comfort or do you prefer a simple beauty routine due to a busy lifestyle? **Anyone can do easy, but you were designed for extraordinary.** If you desire to be a powerhouse influencer, it will require you dress to thrill as sharp as a million-dollar bill.

Does your attire reflect and accurately represent your future self? In Secrets of Power Persuasion for Salespeople, author Roger Dawson stated, "Two questions salespeople ask me a lot is, 'How should I dress, and what image should I project?' The answer is that you should dress well enough that you don't appear to need the sale to survive, but not so well that the buyer can't relate to you. That's where top-quality clothing comes in. It has a quiet elegance about it. There's no question that we are more easily persuaded by people who dress better than we do." Dawson also disclosed that researchers Freed, Chandler, Mouton, and Blake conducted a now-famous experiment on how easy it would be to encourage people to ignore a 'Don't Walk' sign at a city intersection. When a well-dressed individual ignored the sign, 14% of the people had been waiting for the light to change followed him across. When the same person repeated the experiment the next day, now dressed in sloppy clothes, only 4% of the people followed him across.

I recall a businesswoman conducting an initial meeting to discuss a potential project and was prepared to hire an event planner on the spot. The deal breaker was seeing the event planner casually dressed in flip flops; it cost her a $5,000.00 contract. As you step into your awesome, don't leave your fancy clothes behind. Georgio Armani admonished us to be aware that, **"Elegance is not about being noticed, it's about being remembered."** The goal is to always leave an indelible impression that cannot be erased.

Even with all the hocus pocus advertising, multibillion-dollar corporations are spending there is still a select group of women who do not invest extra time in presenting themselves in the brightest light. It can be challenging to shine when you refuse to be refined. Many female leaders state they don't want to wear makeup, put on skirts, have their eyebrows sculpted, etc. This is a personal choice, but it is crucial to understand you could be missing out on countless benefits that come with having a polished look.

When you are determined to put your best pumps forward, make certain that you have a backup plan for the days your spirit is down in the dumps. I was approached by a woman who was extremely frustrated with her personal style. In her own opinion, she felt as if her fashion reflected passivity. **The first step to change is acknowledging there is always room for improvement.** Most of us are familiar with the cliché, "You only get one chance to make a good first impression." How often do we neglect our outer appearance with little regard to those we will be interacting with? We embrace a gamut of excuses in defense of our negligence, such as, I was running late, I had too much to do this morning, I am exhausted, I don't feel like going through the trouble and my personal favorite I am not trying to impress anybody. Why not astound yourself?

As women, we are constantly evolving, and our wardrobe can be a primary indicator of where we are mentally, spiritually, and emotionally. I avidly remember one of my professional mentors saying, "Kristie, always dress against the grain." What does that mean? In the words of the famous Dry Idea antiperspirant commercial, "Never let 'em see you sweat." In order to present your most excellent self, it is important that you make an immovable decision to dress for success.

One afternoon, I noticed a beautifully dressed woman standing in line at a local clothing store. As a licensed image enhancement consultant, I, along with the man in front of me, was dazzled at her appearance. This lady was extremely well put together from head to toe. I heard him grunt under his breath, "umm hmm." She wore a classic black dress that was subtle and form-fitting. Her hair was well-groomed, and her makeup neatly applied. What really grabbed my attention were those bodacious, fishnet pantyhose during the height of summertime. I was thinking, You go, girl. She completed the look, not with a pair of flats but four-inch ankle boot pumps.

If you desire to present yourself in public as a fine piece of art to be admired by onlookers, it doesn't happen by osmosis. Every exquisite painting that has stood the test of time required vision, skill and precision of thought. You are the artist of your image and every day you are presented with a blank canvas to craft a new and intriguing masterpiece.

Let's gaze at three jewels of transformation that are guaranteed to enhance your self-image:

Color me beautiful. If you are seeking to blend in, by all means, wear gloomy gray and boring brown. For those who are ready to live out loud, it's time to infuse your wardrobe with radiant reds, optimistic oranges, gorgeous greens, passionate purples, youthful yellows, and breathtaking blues. In the crevice of every color is a powerful source of energy that will either draw or repel others. Unleash your inner color girl.

Tailor-made is the only way. Every outfit in your closet should fit you like a glove, with the exception of lounging attire. Only the items I feel speak and connect to my unique personality are permitted to remain in my wardrobe. Stay away from oversized shirts as they tend to make you appear unnaturally larger. On the opposite side of the spectrum, it is best to avoid clothing that is too tight. If you have major trouble zones that need to be toned, skin gripping garments not only affect your circulation, but they reveal what should be concealed.

Dress your best. When we look our best, we send an internal message to our brain that says we deserve to receive the best. You were born to shine, so refuse to live beneath the standards of show-stopping sizzle fire. I was always told, excellence is in the details. You are worth the extra time it takes to create a phenomenal expression of who you are and where you are headed.

1) **Exercise for a natural high**. In order to combat mental fatigue, consider frequenting the gym, a brisk walk in the park or fitness by TV. The benefits of physical exercise are endless. It is the gift that gives more than you bargained for. Can you imagine increased energy, more happiness, improved sleep and a fabulous new body to dance in?

2) **Create a staple attire, then alternate tops and bottoms**. In your closet, there should be at least one pair of brown, black, nude and navy-blue high heels, slacks, dresses, and skirts. These are the base colors that are easily complemented by plums, oranges, reds and any hue to create the signature statement you desire to make.

3) **Accentuate your assets with accessories**. Elegance is displayed in simplicity. Be intentional with each accessory to ensure that you complement rather than compete with your overall appearance.

4) **Makeup in minutes.** Select five must-have items in your daily routine for a polished and poised presence that takes less than

fifteen minutes.

1) Apply skin tone matching foundation.

2) Fill in eyebrows with a natural brown powder.

3) Select neutral eye shadow (gold/bronze).

4) Elongate your lashes with two coats of marvelous mascara.

5) Add a favorite lip color as a finishing touch.

5) **Sweet signature smell**. A woman's scent has the power to leave a lasting effect on those she encounters. Choose a fragrance that is soft enough to calm and please the nostrils rather than brash and repulsive. Research shows that men perceive women to weigh less when they are wearing a sweet perfume. Talk about getting slim fast.

Before you step out the door, review this Triple A Game Check List:

- Natural makeup, sculpted brows, lubricated lips

- Hair neatly groomed or put on your favorite wig or a super cute hat

- Clean manicured hands and pedicured feet void of chipped polish

- Skin moisturized especially around elbows, knees, and ankles

- Fresh body scent preferably a soft fragrance that attracts, not repels

- Pleasant breath mints for spontaneous conversations that might arise

- Appropriate attire for body shape and non-distracting undergarments

- Shoes free of scuff marks because they appear old and worn

- Complimentary accessories that add a touch of femininity to your clothing

Showcase your style for where you're going, not where you've been. Decide to dress for the promotion or the future position you seek. Dress for the distinguished gentleman you want to attract.

The most important thing to remember is that your self-image is more important than what others think. The extra time you choose to spend on personal grooming will be well worth it. Don't forget to show off that beautiful smile behind the life-changing decision to go the extra mile. Dress your best and settle for nothing less.

C.P.I.L.L. Confidence Prescription for Progress

Crownfirmation: I am willing to invest the time it takes to look great every single day.

Pause to Ponder: What is the number one reason you've neglected your personal image?

I Celebrate:

Leadership Lesson Learned:

Lifestyle Elevation: Every Day I Will,

Day 7

Elevate

To lift up or make higher, raise in rank or status, improve morally, intellectually, or culturally and ascend from a lower to a higher place or position.

Dear Queen,

You possess the strength to overcome any internal struggle. The hardship you are facing is no match for your resilient comeback. **Greatness is discovered in how many times you rise despite insurmountable obstacles.** Michelle Field expressed candidly that, "A queen knows how to build her empire with the same stones that were thrown at her." It does not matter how long you have felt as if you were buried beneath the dirt. The power of your thoughts can give you the thrust you need to ascend and defy any roadblock standing in your way.

No matter what your situation is saying, stand on the rock of unwavering faith knowing you have unequivocally stepped into a new season. God specializes in turning grains of devastation into grand displays of elevation.

As humans, we house infinite potential in the crevices of our beings. Our innate abilities are often buried under the debris of disappointments, despair, and delayed dreams. The mind is a sophisticated instrument that will perform magnificently in the face of adversity. In order for us to operate at optimal capacity, we must re-train the brain to reign victoriously. Lift your eyes upward because blue skies are calling your name.

I know it would be easy to retreat, but it is imperative that you realize you are stronger than your struggle. The simple truth is, there are numerous individuals who are right where you are. They fought relentlessly to pull themselves out of the pit of darkness and despair.

As leaders who are called to stand valiantly on the front line of battle. It is a very sacrificial and selfless position to undertake. If you find yourself growing weary from the seemingly never-ending character-building tests, don't lose heart.

Consider for a second and ask this question, is a sixty-dollar problem preventing you from discovering a $600,000 solution? Don't allow the complexity of thought to rob you of the simplicity to act. You are not a victim, and it is prime time for you to move from stuck to unstoppable.

- Every moment presents an opportunity to rise, rule, roar, and reign.

- To rise is to audaciously move from a lower position to a higher one.

- To rule is to exercise the ultimate power of thought over any negativity.

- To roar is to release a deep prolonged cry from the depths of your soul.

- To reign is to be queen above every difficulty, adversity, and insecurity.

Be unafraid to fight for what you want and war for what you believe you deserve. Remember who you are and change the game. Your crown is not made of diamonds, but of discipline, dedication, and determination. Your value is priceless, and your potential is limitless.

Here are five keys to elevating your life on a consistent basis:

1) **Map your plan.** If you fail to decide on a destination, how will you recognize which roads to take or identify the endpoint when you arrive? Where do you desire to be in the next three to six months, one to three years, five to seven years, seven to ten years and beyond? It may not be the most entertaining way to spend your time, but proper planning is a vital step towards beholding a prosperous future.

2) **Minimize your distractions.** In today's society, the amount of distractions that consume our minds is astounding. Total focus daily is an absolute must if you strive to reach your goals without delay. If you could only do five action items every day what would they be?

3) **Master your craft.** Successful people do ordinary things uncommonly well. In order to stand out among the masses, be prepared to invest considerable time, energy and finances

throughout your entire life. The joy of learning is a wonderful gift that can be re-opened day after day. Operate as a master of the mundane and do it magnificently.

4) **Magnify your message**. It's your lips' turn in the spotlight and boldly using your voice will cause mountains to quake and islands of fear to shake. We often let our insecurities speak louder than our passion, purpose, and power. Your words carry explosive weight to produce waves of change that can break sound barriers. The world is waiting for you to rise to the call of greatness and share your authentic truth.

5) **Monetize your magnificence**. After you have spent adequate time honing your craft and can stand confidently in your ability to deliver solid results, do not discount or underestimate the value that you contribute to the marketplace. Prepare your portfolio for the opportunities ahead. Escape the shadows of insignificance and give the gift of vivacity.

Massive momentum requires massive movement and total annihilation of every excuse. A deliberate shift, strategy and a keen ability is required to seize success. As a wild-hearted dreamer, I live by the words of Milton Berle, "If opportunity doesn't knock, build a door."

When faced with fear, be of good cheer.

When faced with hate, celebrate.

When faced with doubt, look up and shout.

When faced with adversity, unleash tenacity.

When faced with pain, get back up again.

When faced with lack, roar back and attack.

When faced with loss, remember greatness costs.

C.P.I.L.L. Confidence Prescription for Progress

Crownfirmation: As a crown of fire, I have zero qualms about fighting for my deepest desires. I refuse to bow down to intimidation, stagnation, incapacitation or manipulation. I am deeply committed to daily self-actualization. My name is elevation.

Pause to Ponder: What time-wasting activities are you engaging in? Do you have any scheduled events that can be removed from your calendar which are not beneficial to your long-term vision? Are there any dead-end relationships draining you of energy? If so, who are they and in what ways do they deplete your vibrancy?

I Celebrate:

Leadership Lesson Learned:

Lifestyle Elevation: Every Day I Will,

Day 8

Celebrate

To observe a notable occasion, to notice or honor a day, occasion, or deed.

Dear Queen,

Sparks fly the moment you realize that your entire life is a special occasion. Have you been paying keen attention to all the incredible things happening around you? Cultivating an internal discipline to celebrate every season will create boundless personal fulfillment. **Everywhere you go, your essence goes with you.** Are you going to be the life of the party or the one who zaps the life out of the party?

An attitude of gratitude will pull you out of a tunnel of turmoil when you find it difficult to express thanksgiving. Have you ever found yourself experiencing one loss after another? This is where the rubber meets the road, and you find out what you're made of. One of my favorite quotes says, "Pray hardest when it's hardest to pray." In addition we could add, give hardest when it's hardest to give, love hardest when it's hardest to love, celebrate hardest when it's hardest to celebrate, lead hardest when it's hardest to lead, fight hardest when it's hardest to fight, laugh hardest when it's hardest to laugh and believe hardest when it's hardest to believe. In the strength infusing words of Dr. Martin Luther King, Jr., "Our character is revealed not in moments of convenience but in times of challenge."

It can be difficult to celebrate when you feel as if you are sowing more than you are reaping. As visionaries, we often build our dreams in the clouds of our minds before they ever appear in plain sight. During my darkest days, I find comfort in Habakkuk 3:17-19. The prophet was not going to allow his external situation to dictate his internal stance. He said,

"Though the cherry trees don't blossom

and the strawberries don't ripen,

Though the apples are worm-eaten

and the wheat fields stunted,

Though the sheep pens are sheepless

and the cattle barns empty,

I'm singing joyful praise to God.

I'm turning cartwheels of joy to my Savior God.

Counting on God's Rule to prevail,

I take heart and gain strength.

I run like a deer.

I feel like I'm king of the mountain."

Studies estimate that 93% of repetitive behaviors are driven by our subconscious mind and we have the power to re-train our brain. If you plan to alter your default setting it is vital to recognize your normal response when your world goes haywire.

Do you tend to stick your head in the sand when trouble comes calling? Are you prone to burying your emotions until they implode like a piping hot volcano? Does your mouth spew out non-stop complaints about how dissatisfied you are with your life? Once you pinpoint unhealthy emotions, create a Plan of Wellness (POW) to follow when you are triggered to respond negatively.

This is an example of what a POW attack could be: When I feel myself succumbing to a state of despondency, I will follow a pre-written self-restoration and renewal plan. First, I will take a three-day sabbatical from all social media to detox my spirit. Second, I will commit to reading and listening to positive messages to boost my mood. Third, I will engage in a self-care activity such as a bubble bath or a nature walk. Fourth, I will journal my thoughts, ask soul searching questions and write ten expressions of gratitude each day. Fifth, I will cleanse my body of all toxins and consume only green smoothies or water.

As you develop the devotion to celebrate regardless of what life throws your way it is critical to surround yourself with abundance conscious individuals. The healthiest relationships are mutually beneficial. These are intentionally established, high caliber asset founded connections not deficit centered affiliations. There is a steady flow of give and take where each person is motivated by adding value, inspiring growth and thought-provoking transformation.

The habitual practice of thanksgiving will spawn endless opportunities for thanks-living. A daily journaling example would be:

Today, I am grateful for family and friends. I am grateful for a mind that I've trained to win. I am grateful for a vocation that is exhilarating and not emotionally debilitating. I am grateful for those who have come and gone. I am grateful for a heart that beats strong and hard. I am grateful for my rambunctious dog who stays determined to lick my ear off. I am grateful for every platform that allows me to share the gift of empowerment. I am grateful to my spiritual leader who speaks a soul anchoring word of hope in moments I'm tempted to let go. I am grateful to God for embracing me beyond my faults. I am grateful for where I've transcended from and more importantly where I am ascending to. I am grateful for passion, purpose, perseverance, and power to possess divine promises.'

The best days are only a few paces ahead, keep stepping boldly until you kiss the face of the next level. What are you most grateful for?

On this journey, we have two options: to live in misery or merriment. You can create a wonderful world of joy untold the moment you refuse to put your happiness on hold. Celebrate all that you are and all that you can be. Celebrate the courage to conquer your deepest dreams. Celebrate the joy and beauty bottled up in everyday living. Celebrate the people and places that make your heart sing. Celebrate the milestones and the magnificent moments your personal journey may bring. Leave no room for sorrow. Celebrate the possibilities and potential nestled inside a promising tomorrow.

Imagine reading a letter from your future self, after you've reversed the hurt and revived your shine.

'You carry an uncontainable flame of fire in your heart. I've never seen you happier than you are right now. In your most prolific thoughts, did you ever imagine a smile this wide and a serenity that could run this deep? It has been said, "Life doesn't get

easier, you get stronger." Through the most painful circumstances, you've been graced to demonstrate an unwavering faith and tenacity. What I appreciate most about you is that you refuse to surrender to the enemy of defeat. Your creative and optimistic outlook allows you to see the beauty in the burdens. The hope in the hurt. The power in the pain. The revelation in the rejection. The inspiration in the insufficiency. The dream in the despair. The lesson in the loneliness and the courage in the crisis. What I am most certain of is that mistakes do not define you, they refine you into a priceless work of art. I celebrate all that you are and all that you are becoming, a magnificent masterpiece of healing waters.'

C.P.I.L.L. Confidence Prescription for Progress

Crownfirmation: I take time to celebrate every single blessing in my life. I inhale the power of execution and exhale the draining energy of pitiful excuses. My deepest desire is to construct a life filled with wonders that cannot be fathomed and miracles that cannot be counted. This is my hour; this is my moment, this is my season, this is my time, and I will remain devoted to my divine assignment. I am aware. I am astounding. I am affluent. I am ascending. I am wide awake and choose to celebrate.

Pause to Ponder: As you thoughtfully reflect over the past six months, were there missed opportunities to mark the meaningful moments and make the choice to rejoice? At this time, express appreciation for every setback and successful outcome. What is your personal Plan of Wellness in seven steps or less?

I Celebrate:

Leadership Lesson Learned:

Lifestyle Elevation: Every Day I Will,

Day 9

Acceptance

Regarded favorably or given approval.

Dear Queen,

It is critical that you learn how to love yourself in order to overcome the disease to please. As nurturers, we are innately wired to gratify the wishes of others in exchange for their acceptance of us. Can you honestly answer the question, "What does loving myself better look and feel like?"

For an overachiever, that may mean understanding you don't have to compete for any prize—your best is acceptable. **If you are a mother and a wife trying to keep it together all the time, breathe and unwind, because your best is acceptable.** We see it frequently in the serial entrepreneur, constantly pursuing the next big thing on a shoestring budget. Be at peace; your best is acceptable.

Self-compassion gave me the freedom to accept and embrace my shortcomings. The beauty of being gentle with yourself is that it allows you to be imperfect, to treat yourself with kindness, to validate your own needs, and speak to yourself with self-respect. This is the same type of love we would generously extend to our closest friends and loved ones.

Shame, struggle, and secrets are often barriers to self-acceptance. It is easy to rehearse the pain of our past and play the blame game. **What if you were living proof that a domestic violence victim can live a life of happiness beyond the hurt?** There is a lonely soul fighting suicidal thoughts, and you could be the lifeline in an endless sea of torment.

After enduring years of suffering emotionally, mentally and physically with fibroid tumors I would often cry at night, "I just want my body back." These tumors were growing larger every year and wreaked havoc at the start of each menstrual cycle. When they were surgically removed, there were four scars on my stomach. At that moment, I had to accept a new aspect of myself and embrace each mark as a token of triumph. David Rossi stated that "scars show us where we have been, they do not dictate where we are going."

I was deeply moved after discovering the story of Ronald Stanford, who was sentenced to life in prison after being charged with a double homicide at the age of thirteen. During the time of his interview, he had served twenty-five years and would not be eligible for parole until 100 years of age. His story is a powerful example of acceptance following the negative consequence of a poor choice. Over the course of twenty-four hours, he is only permitted one hour a day outside of his small jail cell for a simulation of freedom. Instead of being angry about his situation, he chooses to be grateful and escape to unknown places in his mind through books. In the midst of an unfortunate predicament, he refused to permit a life sentence the power to imprison his potential. Ronald decided to capitalize on his captivity, how are you exercising your emancipation?

In bone crushing adversity you can awaken grace in the face of gratitude as you dare to turn anguish into acceptance. When the ground feels like sinking sand, think of these words by Paulo Coelho, "Someday we'll forget the hurt, the reason we cried and, who caused us pain. We will finally realize that the secret of being free is not revenge, but letting things unfold in their own way and own time. After all, what matters is not the first, but the last chapter of our life which show how well we ran the race. So, smile, laugh, forgive, believe and love all over again."

If you are battling against self-rejection stand in front of the mirror and remind yourself:

You were created for a significant purpose. Your unique purpose is intended to be an instrumental note of inspiration in the life of someone else. Every experience, whether good or bad, provide testimonies of triumph that will strengthen others who are now where you once were. Dare to become an emblem of hope as you remind yourself, your best is good enough.

1) **Give yourself permission to exit**. It is your free will right to leave the company of anyone whom you deem unappreciative of your valuable time, space and brilliance. We've heard the familiar quote, "To the world, you are one person, but to one person, you are the world." Evolve into someone more beautiful and receive those who treasure your exquisite nature to bask your divine essence.

2) **Find your strength in love**. During the seasons where you question if you are making a significant difference, connect with those who truly recognize, regard and respect the value that you contribute. Additionally, empower your mind with affirmations to rebuild your intestinal vigor. You are destined to leave an eternal imprint that cannot be expunged.

3) **Be courageous and try again**. After you have experienced a serious disappointment, heartbreak or set back this can be most challenging because of the grit and guts you will need to muster up. You must resolve emphatically and unequivocally that you will conquer once more. Your life is not over; it has only just begun. When the going gets tough, the tough must always remember, "Your best is still good enough." Give it your all and never give up.

Acceptance is a vital element of self-transformation which will release you from the rope of self-pity and ensure you remain mentally free. It opens the door to liberty making you free to be, free to conceive new dreams, free to love, free to laugh, free to dance, free to think, free to wonder, free to play, free to slay, free to pray and free to still away. Debbie Ford captures this thought precisely. "When you invoke the agent of change called acceptance, you must accept all that you are, all that you've been, and all that you will be in the future."

There is life in you, so live your life. There is joy in you, so spark joy in your life. There is hope in you, so spread that hope. There is depth in you, so unveil your deepest self. There is peace in you, so be peaceful. There is love in you, so learn to love others. There is wisdom in you, so share your knowledge. There is more in you, so explore. Brace yourself for unfathomable victories. It's going to reign rivers, oceans, and seas of limitless possibilities.

C.P.I.L.L. Confidence Prescription for Progress

Crownfirmation: I am in pursuit of authentic living, fully accepting and loving myself without limits.

Pause to Ponder: What is currently unraveling in your world that you find difficult to accept and what makes it challenging to deal with? Who do you need to become in order to rise above this storm?

I Celebrate:

Leadership Lesson Learned:

Lifestyle Elevation: Every Day I Will,

Day 10

Greatness

Notably large in size, remarkable in magnitude, degree, or effectiveness, distinguished and remarkably skilled.

Dear Queen,

If you asked a hundred people to define greatness, you would probably receive a hundred different answers. The term is highly subjective and guided by our own unique moral compass and human experiences. As a child, I had a picture of Dr. Martin Luther King Jr. on my bedroom wall. He was a symbol of hope, and his passionate speech could burn a hole in the coldest hearts. **When I think of greatness, I believe it is marked by humility and an unwavering dedication to selfless service.** The works of Mother Theresa and Oprah Winfrey have influenced my personal leadership style. We often model the attributes we admire and aspire to attain.

Out of seventeen vision boards displayed in my home office and five vision books, I see this question more than anything. "Are you the best?" It has nothing to do with outside factors. It makes me delve beneath the surface level of my personality. Am I the best at whatever I turn my hands to? Am I the best steward over my time? Am I the best in service to others? Am I the best in communicating a clear, concise and compassionate message? Am I the best at caring for myself? Am I the best friend to those I have a close relationship with? Am I the best in business administration? Am I the best wife to my husband? Am I the best leader I can be? As long as there is breath in my body, the answer will always be no. I will never arrive until I die. I can improve. I can do more. I can step up. I can take one more phone call. I can touch one more heart. I can lay down my pride. I can study five more chapters. I can create a brand-new course because to whom much is given, much is demanded.

Honestly, I never desired to be a leader when I was younger as I was keenly aware it required a lot of work. William Shakespeare stated, "Some are born great, some achieve greatness, and some have greatness thrust upon them."

Every day I elevate my mental state from good to great. A myriad of individuals are disembodied from their divine purpose, which leads to disempowerment, which leads to disappointment, which leads to emotional drain. Decide to stop dismissing your true desires. When you ignore the call to greatness, you are providing a disservice to your propensity to lead.

Let's explore five self-disciplines great leaders do before 8:00 a.m.:

1) **Start early and map out your day.** Love it or hate it, utilizing the morning hours before work may be the key to a successful and healthy lifestyle. That's right, early rising is a common trait found in many CEOs, government officials, and other influential people. Margaret Thatcher was up every day at 5:00 a.m.; Frank Lloyd Wright at 4:00 a.m. and Robert Iger, the

CEO of Disney at 4:30 a.m. just to name a few. I know what you're thinking—you do your best work at night. Not so fast. According to Inc. Magazine, morning people have been found to be more proactive and more productive. In addition, the health benefits for those with a life before work go on and on.

2) **Move your body**. Get your blood circulating, and your mind revved up for a brand-new set of challenges waiting to see if you will fight or fold. Moving your body sends a message to your brain that you are ready to step into a powerful force field of energy that will protect you from negativity.

3) **Eat a healthy breakfast**. The temptation to run out the door on fumes is high for a leader who has an overloaded plate. You need the proper fuel to operate in your optimum state throughout the day. Sugary breads and drinks do not equate to a healthy breakfast. Can you imagine what would transpire if you significantly decreased foods that have low nutritional value in exchange for high-value nutritional foods? You would be less irritated, calm in spirit, have clarity of thought and internally gratified from making choices from an elevated posture.

4) **Visualize your success**. One of the greatest weapons of progress that you possess is the power to visualize. Can you see the successful outcome of a project before the work is done? Can you see your new beach body before the two-piece bikini is ever put on? Can you see the man of your dreams holding you tightly? Can you see the six-bedroom home with

two baths on Sandle Wood Street before you open the door? Can you see the building to your company that serves thousands of clients each month before you file with the Division of Corporations? Walt Disney said, "If you can dream it, you can do it. All our dreams can come true, if you possess the courage to pursue them."

5) **Conquer the mountains before the molehills**. The morning is the time when you are fresh with new ideas and creativity. Therefore, this is the prime time to handle seemingly difficult projects. Sir Edmund Hillary shared this perspective: "It's not the mountain we conquer, it is ourselves." We conquer procrastination, we conquer excuses, we conquer distractions, we conquer inadequacies, and we conquer everything that makes us shrink back.

Yield to greatness, elevation and the sacred awakening of unfathomable transformation. **Come out of hiding and never make your home in the shadows.** Refuse to allow any negative experience to define you. Grant yourself the intergalactic space to evolve into a powerful queen who is strong, confident and free to be.

C.P.I.L.L. Confidence Prescription for Progress

Crownfirmation: Greatness is an extension of who I am and a mirror reflection demonstrating selfless service to others daily.

Pause to Ponder: Who are the top three leaders you respect most and what attributes do you desire to model in your personal leadership style?

I Celebrate:

Leadership Lesson Learned:

Lifestyle Elevation: Every Day I Will,

Day 11

Mindset

A mental attitude or inclination, a fixed state, tendency, or habit.

Dear Queen,

As I look back over the course of my life, I understand that the enemies of my soul were never after my external possessions, but the internal substance which is rooted in my faith to see, believe, and receive. At some point on your journey to greatness, you must draw a line in the sand and come to the end of your rope of dysfunction. How long will you subscribe to a faulty mindset that is ruining your relationships, sabotaging your success, crippling your confidence, frustrating your family, mangling your money, harassing your health, oppressing your opportunities, pulverizing your progress, and vandalizing your vision?

What will it take for you to defend your potential against fear, doubt, procrastination, laziness and everything else in between? The hour has come for you to stop with every excuse as to why you are unable to achieve your dreams. If you have breath in your body, you are ready. C. Joy Bell said there are two things we should always be:

1) Raw

2) Ready

When you are raw, you are always ready, and when you are ready, you usually realize that you are raw. Waiting for perfection is not an answer, one cannot say "I will be ready when I am perfect" because then you will never be ready, rather one must say "I am raw, and I am ready just like this right now, how and who I am."

Let's peer into a comprehensive landscape of what the word ready entails:

- To be fully organized and prepared

- In a suitable state for an activity, action or situation

- Available for service or progress

- Willing to do something

- Equipped for what is about to occur

In order to posture yourself for advancement and accomplishment, it will require an acutely focused frame of mind for what is on the horizon. **This is commonly referred to as vision.** Are you able to see beyond your current situation into a future blossoming with bourgeoning possibilities?

If you have been feeling frazzled, frustrated and flustered over thoughts of stagnancy and sheer complacency now is your split-second moment to shake the dust of mediocrity off your mind.

Decide to divorce the darkness of defeat and place yourself in a prime position to seize the sunlight of success. Anyone can talk readiness, but it takes daily discipline to be and stay ready for unseen opportunities that await your emergence.

As you adjust your internal compass, take a few minutes to evaluate to see if you are as prepared as you think you are. To play a bigger game on a higher plane, here are six questions to consider:

1) **Are you organized and prepared for your next big move?** Are you able to clearly perceive the direction in which you are heading? At the beginning of transition, we go through a gathering phase where we lay out the puzzle pieces for strategic placement. This is when you are writing out specific plans and developing detailed ideas. Who do you aspire to partner with on a proposed venture? What does your visual imagery look like? Who will design your marketing materials? What is the concise message you desire to convey? To whom will you be directly speaking to?

2) **Is your thought process in a suitable state for next level living?** If you are combating strong emotions pertaining to self-doubt, it will be quite difficult to operate at an accelerated pace and ascend to higher dimensions of brilliance. Pursuing your passion and purpose is no simple feat. It will challenge every fiber of your being and require nothing less than blood, sweat, and tears. There is no room for fear.

3) **Can you contribute time, energy and resources to a cause bigger than yourself?** I recently read a profound quote by Tony Gaskins that stated, "The doors will be open to those who are bold enough to ask." Opportunities often elude us

because we appear unavailable in our dispositions and slothful in attack.

4) **Are you willing to work hard with or without reward?** At the budding of a dream, you may have to invest countless hours and lose precious sleep before ever experiencing monetary payoffs. That is why it's vital that you seek that which brings you the greatest fulfillment within. This will become the fuel necessary to keep your fire blazing during seasons of mental fatigue and weariness.

5) **Are you equipped to proficiently operate in what is about to occur?** If you are a singer, you should have at least several songs that you are primed to sing on the spot with or without a music band and background singers. Are you a speaker? If a company was to inquire about hiring you, do you have a speaker's reel, one-sheet or a signature message available to submit?

6) **Be prepared for change.** In the words of Jim Rohn, business philosopher, "When you change, everything changes." Anything we attain in life is sheer proof of the action steps we put in motion.

I have discovered four phases of mindset evolution during the process of dream development.

Phase one: I want to be a _____. (Fill in the blank.)

Phase two: I will be a _____. (Fill in the blank.)

Phase three: I work to be a _____. (Fill in the blank.)

Phase four: I am a _____. (Fill in the blank.)

It is important that you find out where you are in your own journey towards greatness. The possibilities are infinite.

C.P.I.L.L. Confidence Prescription for Progress

Crownfirmation: I will protect and shield my mind from every voice of negativity.

My mind is powerful.

My mind is sacred.

My mind is pure.

My mind is expansive.

My mind is magnificent.

My mind is limitless.

My mind is explosive.

My mind is strong.

My mind is fortified.

My mind is unbreakable.

My mind is unshakable.

My mind is unstoppable.

Pause to Ponder: Where can you eliminate complexity from your own life? Describe in your own words how it feels to be aligned with who you were created to be? How is life different now that you confidently know where you are going?

I Celebrate:

Leadership Lesson Learned:

Lifestyle Elevation: Every Day I Will,

Day 12

Consistency

A pattern of sticking with one way of thinking or acting agreement or harmony between parts or elements.

Dear Queen,

How do you intend to ascend to altitudes of astounding affluence when your adverse attitude is affixed in the abyss of apathy? **Do you find yourself constantly postponing important commitments, goals, and aspirations?** I've experienced quite often the very thing that I prolonged starting required less than an hour to complete. If we desire to eradicate the habitual pattern of procrastination, we must first be aware of the faulty thought processes adopted over the course of our lives.

Why do countless individuals succumb to mediocrity and apathy? Having the creative finesse to dream a million dreams is easy. The real challenge arises the second you realize that true change requires relentless effort and an unwavering commitment before you experience the fulfillment of your personal desires. It has been stated that the world is run by tired men. If you want to accomplish anything noteworthy, it will be imperative to do whatever it takes to make it happen. Anything of value is a byproduct of constant discipline, dedication, and determination.

Consistency is one of the major keys you need to succeed. Procrastination is a master thief of productivity. A few basic definitions of procrastination are:

To defer action, to put off until another day or time, to do nothing, postponing something, to be slow or late about doing something that should be done and the habit of putting off.

Numerous individuals fantasize over the idea of starting a business, writing a book or simply ascending the corporate ladder of achievement. Yet, at the first sign of opposition, distractions, and disappointments they collapse under the weight of pressure.

Over the past several years, after major surgery, I have been extremely intentional about my personal health and wellness. The transformational process is a never-ending battle and consistency of focus is a perpetual challenge. I have established success plans to ensure I remain unyielding in my progress. Have you ever heard the saying, "If you fail to plan, you plan to fail."?

In order to win in wellness, I have several coloring books for art therapy that allow me to decompress from the complexity of business building. I affirm myself with positive words of inspiration. I am surrounded by seventeen vision boards. I empty my negative thoughts and priceless moments in my journal. I exercise frequently with cardio dance and weightlifting. I take nature walks to slow down when I begin to feel overly anxious, and I visit the day spa for massages or a soothing manicure/pedicure. These are a few behind the scenes activities that I do consistently. The top characteristic that I am frequently complimented on is my high energy, and it is a result of doing these simple things that keep me emotionally happy.

One question I am repeatedly asked is, "How do you continually maintain your passion and drive?" For me, it is **not a matter of maybe** I will pursue my purpose, it is a **matter of must**. Every person must resolve within themselves to relentlessly pursue their individual life goals. It may take a year, or it may take ten years. However long it takes, don't stop moving forward until the vision within is apparent to all. I believe this type of unyielding commitment is what separates the haves from the have nots. Every amount of success is a mere reflection of your tenacious efforts to ascend beyond the narrow confines of mediocrity.

I challenge you to push beyond any self-imposed limitations that arise from the crevices of your mind. Your future success will be directly influenced by the actions you execute on a daily basis. The crowning victories that await your arrival are predicated on you purposefully choosing to exceed your greatest expectations and those of non-contributing spectators. Always remember, in the words of Ralph Marston, "You make your own odds. Stack them 100% in your favor."

The power to be is in the will to do. Now is the perfect moment to make it happen, no matter what steps you have to take. **Everything you were designed to accomplish and achieve is within arms' reach**. The life you've been dreaming of is waiting patiently at your front door. Don't ever settle for less when the field of dreams has adequate space to provide you with more land to explore.

We have a tendency to sabotage our individual progress in search of the perfect set of circumstances, which are rarely available.

To eradicate procrastination, you must:

1) Take full ownership of your personal responsibilities.

2) Establish a daily to-do list and exceed written expectations.

3) Tackle the least favorable tasks at the onset of each new day for peak performance.

It is essential that we grow as we go towards success and prosperity. I challenge you to become an unstoppable force of motion. When you begin to feel overwhelmed with the demands of life, remember to slay, don't delay.

C.P.I.L.L. Confidence Prescription for Progress

Crownfirmation: I will cultivate an appetite for greatness and refuse to consume the bitter fruit of frustration. I will search for the crown of compassion and refuse to hold the horns of hatred. I will rest in the arms of infinite freedom and refuse to live in a prison of procrastination. I will celebrate the beauty of life and refuse to merely exist as a float drifting along the tides. I will fight for a brighter tomorrow and refuse to doubt that anything is possible.

There is no problem I cannot solve. There is no barrier I cannot overcome. There is no force that can stand against the truth. There is absolutely no limit to what I can do.

Pause to Ponder: What is one new habit you can practice consistently and take action persistently towards each day?

I Celebrate:

Leadership Lesson Learned:

Lifestyle Elevation: Every Day I Will,

Day 13

Obscurity

The state of being unknown or forgotten or something that is difficult to understand.

Dear Queen,

The word *Sawubona* is an African Zulu greeting which means, "I see you." I see your personality." I see your humanity. I see your dignity. I see your beauty. I see your brilliance. I see your power. In response, the person who was warmly greeted says, *Ngikhona*, meaning, "I am here."

There is a distinct difference between being hidden and hiding. The first is rooted in preparation and the latter trepidation. I've come to learn that I must take authority and then crush fear. When I bend to fear what transpires next is my hopes, dreams, and goals are held captive by false illusions. I don't know how much time I wasted in my youth or how many opportunities were left on the table because of my hesitation to come out of the shadows of obscurity, pivot into power and step onto the stage of greatness. The key to overcoming your fear is fortified focus and unshakeable faith. Michelle Schaper described it superbly when she said, "She wears a crown built from her spine of inner strength and modesty with sparkling jewels to represent each of her divine qualities of eminence."

I've learned that my greatest ally is adversity and my most powerful nemesis is comfort. One of my favorite quotes states that nothing great ever occurred in the comfort zone. I used to run from the call to leadership. Remaining in the background was undeniably safe. There is no accountability or responsibility and no pressure to perform continuously especially under daunting life challenges. Yet, I was always craving for more. I remember during the eight years of being employed as a secretary while walking to work I would say out loud, "There has to be more to life than this. Something has to give." As I look back in retrospect, that something was me. I was standing in my own way of success the entire time. Talk about a blind spot. During times of hardship, I would say to myself, **"I can live magnificently in the face of adversity."** One of my mentors told me early in the genesis of my entrepreneurial journey, "Never allow money to dictate what you can or cannot have or do. Never say quit and never say die." The tough times taught me how to ascend from within and win again and again. As long as the fire inside of you remains greater than the fire on the outside, you can awaken from the ashes of obscurity and rise.

Do you open your eyes in the morning filled with hopefulness or hopelessness? This is important because how you approach each day sets a precedent for how adept you will be at solving the problems that come your way. We are afforded an opportunity to showcase new dreams, skills and a winning attitude as a new sun rises to greet us. It takes creative insight to make every moment our masterpiece.

I am reminded of Job's response to his wife during a season of hardship and despair.

"You speak as one of the foolish women. What? Shall we accept only good at the hand of God and shall we not accept misfortune and what is of a bad nature? In spite of all this, Job did not sin with his lips."

– Job 2:10

In life, we will be extended a buffet of experiences. Most people don't naturally crave cauliflower over candy, yet we need the nutritional value that is derived from our vegetables. The disappointments of life are our spiritual vegetables, if you desire to be strong and healthy you must consume them.

Many individuals are carrying more than one dream in their hearts and have endured countless opposition while waiting for their arrival. I hold these sweet words spoken by former First Lady Eleanor Roosevelt close to my heart, "The future belongs to those who believe in the beauty of their dreams." **It is easy to let go of a dream, but it takes courage, tenacity and unyielding resolve of the will to hold on to that which seems impossible**. In the mirror's hollow, cascading thoughts of what you deem yourself to be is a vivid reflection of a divine ability to see what others may not, cannot or will not perceive.

Have you placed your dreams on the shelf? Have you lost hope? Have you thrown in the towel? Are you afraid to take a leap of faith due to a fear of what happened before or what could happen if you dare, decide and do? Are you aware that one of the best ways to overcome the fear of failure is by having the unrelenting audacity to dream bigger and brighter in the midst of dark grey skies and tear-filled eyes?

You must learn how to work in the dark. Dark is defined as difficult to interpret, lacking brightness, disheartening and is military lingo for sudden termination of communication. If you find yourself walking through the valleys of the shadows of death, fear no evil. Quiet the outside world and listen to the still small voice of wisdom that lives within saying, Rise again. H. Norman Wright said, "Some people are like medieval castles. Their high walls keep them safe from being hurt. They protect themselves emotionally by permitting no exchange of feelings with others. No-one can enter. They are secure from attack. However, inspection of the occupant finds him or her lonely, rattling around the castle alone. The castle dweller is a self-made prisoner. He or she needs to feel loved by someone, but the walls are so high that it is difficult to reach out or for anyone else to reach in." After the hype, get alone and hone your focus, your faith, and your fight. In times of uncertainty, there is still work to be done, life to be lived, roses to smell and love to be shared.

If you won't be faithful to build in obscurity how can you be trusted to reign in notoriety? Nations shall come to your light and kings to the brightness of your dawn. When the invitations to elevation arrive are you prepared to accept them?

Throughout the sands of time, we have read fascinating accounts of high caliber women who possessed a powerful and commanding presence at the entrance of any scene they entered. Their mysterious and admirable qualities are available to many but only embodied by those who commit to a lifetime of growth investment. What are the dynamic characteristics of attention-grabbing shine? How can you awaken the sleeping beauty within and bring her alive?

Our motto in beauty school was, "Beauty is as beauty does." Unfortunately, today's media focuses primarily on women acting out of character rather than exemplifying ladylike behavior. A true queen has learned how to remain poised under pressure. She rarely allows her feathers to be ruffled in retaliation. This queen would rather showcase the splendor of calm in chaos. An authentic queen knows how to gracefully be at the center of attention yet remain thoughtfully aware of all who are in the midst of her glowing gaze. She is meticulously put together as if every aspect of her person was carefully planned before making a public appearance. The words uttered from her lips evolve from the laws of kindness, and her mind is razor sharp ready for any test that requires her to showcase her cleverness. The apparel she selects is distinctive, timeless and guaranteed to make a lasting statement. Her delicate frame is garnished with class and style. This regal crown prefers respect over disdain, authority over insecurity, love over hatred, diligence over slothfulness and magnificence over mediocrity.

It only takes a moment to make a moment. In life, every end has a new beginning. Go for the bold colors, go for the front row and go for the wild adventures that have yet to be told. Let the miraculous unfold meticulously, masterfully and magnetically. Turn on your shine and never hide because the world needs more of your sparkling light.

Choose to run your race at your own pace with divine grace. Always remember, hopeful hearts can't help but glitter. Start extracting treasures from the inner turmoil and pick the tulips from your trouble with confidence knowing you can walk with your head high in triumph despite trauma and travesty. Free yourself from the desert of obscurity, pick up your crown and never sit it down on the ground.

C.P.I.L.L. Confidence Prescription for Progress

Crownfirmation: Every negative emotion follows my command. I have the power to bring any thought into captivity as I walk gracefully in the spirit of victory.

Pause to Ponder: What gifts of greatness are you hiding and allowing to remain dormant as a result of not feeling good enough to share with others? How different would you and your life be if you chose to courageously lower the brass barriers and open your heart freely?

I Celebrate:

Leadership Lesson Learned:

Lifestyle Elevation: Every Day I Will,

Day 14

Fortify

To make strong and secure, to give physical strength, courage, or endurance to.

Dear Queen,

Can you imagine being stranded amidst the desert sands without food or water, your body scorching hot from the burning sun and your mind weary from a grueling journey? Why do people choose to surrender to pain as they plumb the depths in the darkest nights of their plight? Frequently succumbing to hopelessness just before the dawn gives way to light? On the opposite end of a vacillating pendulum stands a group of iron-willed warriors who choose to fight and not faint, rise and not retreat, soar and not sink.

Do you struggle to find calm in the center of chaos? The naked truth is everyone experiences challenges throughout different junctures in life. How do you remain composed when it seems as if the weight of the world is resting upon your shoulders? **If you desire to thrive during arid dry times, it is essential that you learn to adapt like a chameleon and change with your circumstances.**

When you are confronted with hardship and your strength begins to fade that is the exact moment to expect an oasis of opportunity to flood you with pleasure despite the unrelenting aches. An oasis is a place of happiness in the midst of trouble or difficulty. Until you learn how to subdue the tropical storm brewing on the inside, you will never be able to conquer the tsunami raging on the outside.

A winning attitude merely boils down to a matter of perspective. Recently, I read a quote that stated, "When you change the way you look at things, the things you look at change." The bottom line is apathy has no power to move mountains.

The tale of two salesmen is one of my token mindset stories. One version reads: Many years ago, two salesmen from very different companies were sent to a remote third-world island, to find out if there was any market for shoe sales. Upon arrival, they each noticed that none of the locals were wearing shoes. They were all barefooted. Salesman number one immediately contacted his office headquarters, and said, "This is terrible. No-one here wears shoes. There is no market here." Salesman number two also called his company promptly, and said, "This is fantastic. No-one here wears shoes. There is a huge market here, and the possibilities are endless."

Refuse to forfeit your power, the ability to act in the desert of discomfort. You were born to be a victor, not a victim. Always remember, there is strength in your struggle.

If you have the courage to chase a dream, you will need the fortitude to find that dream.

You are not fragile; you are a fortified city.

You are not a failure; you are a phenomenal masterpiece.

You are not forgotten, you are a force to be reckoned with.

Do not cast away your confidence; it will produce great rewards in the end. You must live to tell the story of how you hammered down the hurdles that were positioned to stop you.

Breathe again, reach again, live again, fight again, hope again, dream again, believe again and do whatever it takes to move again.

> "Muster every ounce of strength within you and fight. Your life is worth it, your future is worth it, and your destiny is worth it. Fortitude is the Marshall of thought, the armor of the will, and the fort of reason."
>
> –Francis Bacon

Do not allow your feelings to fool you, let them fuel you forward. If you feel tired, remember you are triumphant. If you feel weak, remember you are a warrior. If you feel fragile, remember you are a fortress. If you feel confused, remember you are more than a conqueror. If you feel lost, remember you are a leader. If you feel rejected, remember you are a ruler. If you feel voiceless, remember you are victorious. Remember who you are and change the game.

The first step in gaining fortitude is to ask yourself, "What do I value most? What do I fear losing the most?"

> "The brave person values the thing he is pursuing more than the thing he is risking."
>
> –Unknown

When I find myself weary from the fight of life I run to the words of Rocky Balboa, "Let me tell you something you already know. The world ain't all sunshine and rainbows. It is a very mean and nasty place, and it will beat you to your knees and keep you there permanently if you let it. You, me, or nobody is gonna hit you as hard as life. But it ain't how hard you hit; it's about how hard you can get hit, and keep moving forward. How much you can take and keep moving forward? That's how winning is done. Now, if you know what you're worth, then go out and get what you're worth. But you gotta be willing to take the hit, and not pointing fingers saying you ain't where you are because of him, or her, or anybody. Cowards do that and that ain't you. You're better than that."

You were given this mountain to show others that it can be moved. There are more for you than against you. Fear has no power unless you yield to it. Release the roar and overcome every obstacle. Be resolute and keep your eyes on your own prize because it's majestic.

Fortify your spirit with the big picture, focus your mind on the prize and fiercely cross the finish line with all your might. Stop searching for a solution and become the answer. You are needed. You are important. Your life matters.

C.P.I.L.L. Confidence Prescription for Progress

Crownfirmation: I am an unshakeable mountain of strength. I have one of the most brilliant minds in the universe. My cognitive ability is razor edge sharp.

Pause to Ponder: The question you fear to ask will result in a single answer never to be grasped. Why do you doubt the power you possess?

I Celebrate:

Leadership Lesson Learned:

Lifestyle Elevation: Every Day I Will,

Day 15

Overwhelm

To cause someone to have too many things to deal with or to defeat someone completely.

Dear Queen,

Have you found yourself in a spiritual drought, feeling as if you have nothing left to give out? I have good news, from the depths of your belly shall flow rivers of living water. During my quiet time alone I began to contemplate what would cause a river, which is a powerful force of nature to dry up completely?

Typically, when the climate changes and the temperature rises, it can cause a rapid racing river to transform into dry land. Therefore, it is essential to nurture your spirit in the best of times and in the worst of times. Another reason a river dries up is if it is dependent on rainfall. This could equate to you looking for an outside source of support to water your internal needs. Lastly, one of the most common justifications of depletion is overuse. When the demand exceeds the supply, you will find yourself completely dry.

It seems as if today's ambitious women are seeking to attain a gold medal for exhaustion. I will never forget the words of a woman who was at her wit's end: "I. Am. Tired. I feel as if my brain and body are shutting down. I've been dealing with this situation for over a year.

The stress has overwhelmed me." At that moment, I reminded her that there is strength in numbers. If one can chase a thousand, two can put ten thousand to flight. The diabolical plan of your invisible enemy is for you to isolate not collaborate. Understand this, no matter how difficult the fight or how dark the night you were not created to live in a bubble. Wonder Woman, drop the act. You deserve to breathe deeply, happily and freely.

As I glance through the corridors of time reflecting on my never-ending personal journey to greatness, admittedly there are days that I am moved to tears. My heart is full of gratitude under the simmering truth that I chose to rise above the storms of life. I refused to give up on myself, in the presence of infinite reasons to quit. I crawled through the valleys of the shadow of death with victory encapsulated in the palm of my hands.

Recently, I read a quote that stated, **"Everything that you're going through is preparing you for what you've asked for."** Many individuals fail to ascend to unimaginable heights when they cower and run from the alarming trumpet sounds of adversity.

Can you imagine if every tree on earth uprooted itself in response to the howling winds of inclement weather? How chaotic would the entire world be? A champion's spirit is extraordinarily equipped with an internal fortitude and trained to remain unmoved by any daunting opposition.

Will hardship feel good? No. Will it make you uncomfortable? Yes. Everyone can shine bright like a diamond if they are willing to go through the process of being cut and fashioned into a resplendent work of art.

At the intersection of change, a split-second decision shattered my limited perspective in an instant and the call to destiny could no longer be resisted. **One of the most profound moments of my existence was the day I granted myself permission to define and design the life I deserved on my own terms.**

I allowed myself a sacred space to imagine and voyage where anything was possible if I believed. In this place, I am fully cognizant that where I am, is not where I will always be. I am acutely aware of the power that I possess. In my left ear I hear, the words of Eleanor Roosevelt whisper loud and clear, "No-one can make you feel inferior without your consent." In my right, I muse on the thoughts of Lena Horne, "It's not the load that breaks you down, it's the way you carry it." I am not alone. I bear in my soul a billion allies.

Are you sinking deep in an ocean of overwhelm? Do you feel like the little hamster on a wheel, exerting precious energy to no avail? Let's be candid. During times of frustration it is easy to lose perspective on the primary objective. If we cultivate a breeding ground for negative emotions, a perpetual cycle of undesirable outcomes will be harvested. When your back is against the wall, it is essential to focus on leveraging internal power to fuel forward.

Only in Utopia would we all live together in perfect harmony with not a single problem waiting for us to solve. Reality as we know is coupled with simplicities and complexities. That which comes to challenge us is often the catalyst to prepare us for greater milestones ahead. "The beautiful thing about transformation is that it welcomes us to experience something new each and every day."

Until you learn how to master your emotions and motivate yourself beyond the pit of despair into the palace of destiny, stagnancy will be your tarnishing reward. Anyone can express the desire for change but how many are willing to invest countless hours in order to create change?

Three ways win the war against overwhelm are:

1) **Avoid continuously reiterating an offense, hurt or disappointment to those closest to you.** It has been said that interfering with a wound will delay healing. Do not allow yourself to become paralyzed by a single moment that will become a distant memory.

2) **Detox from the inside out.** Select healthier meals that make you glow from within. Meditate on positive words of affirmation that build your confidence level, one thought at a time. Get physically fit while dropping pounds of pressure off the top of your shoulders.

3) **Celebrate love, lessons, and laughter as the pages turn in each chapter of your life.** I have adopted this mantra: That which you appreciate, appreciates. When you concentrate on what is true, lovely and virtuous, a habitation of goodness will become your emotional safe haven.

Take another look in the mirror and appreciate just how far you've come. The beautiful life you've created did not come easy, yet you are still standing tall. It's amazing how much you've transformed right before your very eyes from mirror to manifestation. You must be astonished at the courage you display every day to take a bigger bite out of life.

Carve out a special time to regroup, reflect and restore your empty cup until it once again overflows. Continue to speak what you seek to be unleashed. No-one has to publicly affirm you because you already have spoken well of yourself privately. Stay strong, stay sharp, stay out of the shadows and show up relentlessly authentic. You are powerful and your galactic ideas will produce a gargantuan impact. Today you need rest because tomorrow will demand a new roar.

Finally, in the words of Mother Theresa who left a priceless legacy of love:

People are often unreasonable, illogical and self-centered;

Forgive them anyway.

If you are kind, people may accuse you of selfish, ulterior motives;

Be kind anyway.

If you are successful, you will win some false friends and some true enemies;

Succeed anyway.

If you are honest and frank, people may cheat you;

Be honest and frank anyway.

What you spend years building, someone could destroy overnight;

Build anyway.

If you find serenity and happiness, they may be jealous;

Be happy anyway.

The good you do today, people will often forget tomorrow;

Do good anyway.

Give the world the best you have, and it may never be enough;

Give the world the best you've got anyway.

You see, in the final analysis, it is between you and God;

It was never between you and them anyway.

C.P.I.L.L. Confidence Prescription for Progress

Crownfirmation: I am on the cusp of embracing my greatest accomplishments. I am pregnant with possibilities, full of boundless potential waiting to be unleashed.

Pause to Ponder: When was the last time you felt overwhelmed and what was the underlying cause? What three actions can you take to shift from your negative state to a more liberating place of peace?

I Celebrate:

Leadership Lesson Learned:

Lifestyle Elevation: Every Day I Will,

Day 16

Game Changer

An event, idea, or procedure that effects a significant shift in the current manner of doing or thinking about something.

Dear Queen,

Until you ascertain how to produce more than you pout, the likelihood of you becoming a powerhouse is unquestionably a long shot. The term game changer is packed with powerful meaning as it provokes one to consider whether they are merely watching from the sidelines of life or out on the field working hard to successfully win the game they're in.

Most often, game changers are clearly recognized as our thought leaders, chief executive officers, entrepreneurs and inventors who create a global shift through technological advancements. They have an uncanny ability to disrupt the entire course of history by one phenomenal event built upon years of consistent action steps.

As a result of this new path developed by an innovative trailblazer, others are fueled with inspiration to believe they too can transform the world in an impactful way. **In order to be a game changer, it will require that you become comfortable being unique.** When I was young my wild personality stood out everywhere I went. I was not trying to be different, but my carefree disposition was easily noticed.

After experiencing social rejection, there was a season where I turned my light almost completely off. Those were the darkest years of my existence because I was not being true to who I was designed to be. I decided to be relentlessly authentic and to never hide.

Any person who wants to be proficient in a specific area of study will begin to research every aspect of the matter until the information can be synthesized. The next step is to add their distinctive perspective to the conversation. There are billions of people in the world. Are you aware of the exceptional attributes that only you can bring to the table? Investors are not fascinated with generic sameness; they are ready to place their money on that which is inimitable or irreplaceable.

If you are ready to revolutionize the game and not simply play the game, consider developing these behavioral proficiencies:

1) **Think differently.** As a leader, you must be comfortable with thinking outside normal organizational paradigms. In order to create dynamic products, services, and solutions it is essential that you are willing to shatter unprofitable business models, strategies and networks.

2) **Take calculated risks.** As you count the cost of each possible opportunity presented, ask yourself the question, "Am I willing to invest time, resources, finances, and mental energy continuously until the desired outcome is achieved?"

3) **Turn crisis into creativity.** Are you able to cultivate creative ideas in the midst of chaotic crises that arise unexpectedly? It is critical to have emotional stability as a game changer because

your mind is the captain of every move to be made.

4) **Talk to game changers**. We all have an individual race to run and must do so at our own pace. During low moments, we gain strength from the momentum of other game changers that will catapult us to heights we may have never attained. Collaboration is an instrumental key that holds the power to unlocking dormant potential waiting to be released.

5) **Transform lives**. Focus on the true purpose of being a game changer, which is simply to transform lives. We are in the business of infusing fresh insights, possibilities, and perspectives into barren minds ready to come alive and thrive.

"Progress is impossible without change, and those who cannot change their minds cannot change anything."

–George Bernard Shaw

You must dream bigger, or you are bound to go backward. You must live larger, or you will lean into little. You must reach higher, or you will suffocate your inner fire. You must love deeper, or you will drift alone in a shallow existence. You must fight harder, or you will faint in the day of adversity. You must believe and only believe, or you will sink beneath the sands of impossibility.

C.P.I.L.L. Confidence Prescription for Progress

Crownfirmation: I will supersede my highest expectancy and excel with acute proficiency in all that is placed before me. The ability to transform is readily available and at my immediate disposal. As I choose to change, so does everything that encompasses me.

Pause to Ponder: How will you change the game in your professional career industry? In your household? In your neighborhood? In your spiritual community? In your relationships? In your physical being? In your leadership?

I Celebrate:

Leadership Lesson Learned:

Lifestyle Elevation: Every Day I Will,

Day 17

Success

To a higher degree, the accomplishment of an aim and the attainment of profit.

Dear Queen,

The vision of success I vividly painted on a canvas of faith in my younger years was colored with large bank accounts, a private jet, gated estate, and luxury vehicles to drive my cares away. Successful living is fueled by mission-driven goals that will leave a significant mark on future generations. The basic definition of success is the accomplishment of achieving a desired goal. In the words of late business philosopher Jim Rohn, "Success is not to be pursued; it is to be attracted by the person you become."

Do you ever sit and wonder about the success secrets of various individuals? How can they accomplish tons of work in a succinct period of time? How did they rise to the top 5% in their class or field of employment? These overachievers have invested years of study in developing a winning mindset in order to become influential, innovative and an impactful force of good in this world. If you study the practices of countless leaders who shine brilliantly in their area of expertise there are five common characteristics they each exemplify:

1) **Vision.** The ability to behold the invisible future during the present time as you move toward an intangible goal established

in your heart and mind. The power to visualize is realized through cultivating the discipline to perceive beyond what is standing in front of your eyes.

2) **Commitment.** The indomitable will to do what must be done whether you feel like it or not. In spite of unfavorable circumstances, the committed person understands that the fortune is in the follow-up. In order to maintain momentum, you must decide that losing your drive or internal thrust is not an option. As a leader, it is critical that you become master of your emotions or they will enslave you.

3) **Passion.** The fuel to propel you beyond mediocrity into mountainous heights of magnificence. Those who dare to leave a lasting legacy and create waves of transformation are ignited by the flames of fire burning in their souls. It is seen in unquenchable hunger or the heart that beats faster, stronger and longer.

4) **Self-Motivation.** The continence to hold oneself to the highest standards of excellence with or without outside support. These individuals understand that success rises and falls on their own two shoulders. They have adopted a mindset that says, "If it's to be, it's up to me." For the self-motivated, there is no vacancy for limitations or procrastination.

5) **Lifelong Learning.** The insatiable thirst to understand the depths of a subject matter and the patience to excavate hidden wisdom for an unspecified amount of time is a must.

Exceptional leaders are dedicated to feeding their mind high-quality concepts on a daily basis. The more you know, the more you grow and the more you grow, the more it shows.

Now is the perfect moment for you to dust off the dirt of defeat because you were not created to lose but fashioned to win big.

I see you smiling brighter than ever before, and yes happiness looks good on you. Cherish this moment and don't ever let it go. Every day you are invited to run tiptoe through the tulips of triumph. Tell me, adventurous one, what do you desire to do next? The world is yours to explore. No limits, no lack, and no laziness have the power hold you back. What got you here will not be enough to get you there. It's time to ascend once again in mind, body, spirit, and soul if you desire to embrace the land of more. Take off the seatbelt of inhibition and prepare for a grand expedition into new horizons.

Did you think life would be this good outside of the cocoon? Freedom is hot couture, and you wear it well. A woman of style, sophistication, and substance. **Beautiful girl, you can do hard things.** I honestly don't think you give yourself enough credit for the ways you effortlessly manifest invisible ideas into tangible inspiration. Never consent to creep when you've been called to soar. Don't you dare stop dancing with destiny, skating into the arms of success, leaping into the lap of luxury and glowing in the face of greatness.

I was asked the question, "What have you sacrificed for success?" I knew the answer immediately. Of course, I had to scratch my itch and start researching the definition of sacrifice. It has several meanings:

1) Surrendering a possession as an offering to God.

2) The act of giving up something else for the sake of a better cause.

3) Something valuable that you decide not to have in order to get something that is more important.

4) To give up something that is valuable to you in order to help another person.

My response was I have sacrificed who I once was in order to become who I was destined to be. I sacrificed fear in exchange for courage. I sacrificed procrastination in exchange for productivity. I sacrificed pain in exchange for purpose. I sacrificed false humility in exchange for bold confidence. I sacrificed an 8 to 5 job in exchange for embracing my dream life. I sacrificed friends of comfort in exchange for accountability partners. I sacrificed mediocrity in exchange for magnificence in motion. I sacrificed the norm in exchange for walking on waters. I sacrificed predictability in exchange for passionate pursuit towards a divine promise. I sacrificed self in exchange for good success.

Are you willing to sacrifice the lesser for the greater?

C.P.I.L.L. Confidence Prescription for Progress

Crownfirmation: As I purpose to commit and persist in the achievement of my goals, success is imminent. I lead with excellence, efficiency and expansive mindedness in everything.

Pause to Ponder: What reoccurring negative thoughts do you need to disengage from in order to reignite your passion for progress?

I Celebrate:

Leadership Lesson Learned:

Lifestyle Elevation: Every Day I Will,

Day 18

Radiance

A quality of brightness and happiness that can be seen on a person's face a warm, soft light that shines from something.

Dear Queen,

Imagine stepping in front of the mirror and seeing your own face smiling back at you. With a deep breath, you open your mouth to say, "Look at me N.O.W. Look at me, W.O.W Never again, will I allow myself or others to dull my shine, steal my power or make me cower, but I will stand erect as a tower. I am a force to be reckoned with. Limitless living is my new norm as I unashamedly take the world by storm."

I see you shining in your new happy, hopeful and healed skin. You've tapped into the essence of royal radiance. Soaked in the oil of gladness not the cloak of madness. Yeah, this right here is what good living and great loving are all about. It is a beautiful sight when you can laugh uncontrollably with yourself and by yourself for no apparent reason. The pictures on the walls of your heart used to look quite different. A simple reminder to you, your energy is contagious, and it does not belong to you alone.

I keep mulling over one of the lines in the movie, Greater. It has sparked a new appreciation of my own personal journey. The coach asked Brandon, "Two people have $10,000. The first one had it given to him and the second one had to work hard to attain it. Which one would be better off?"

After reading a portion of Get Yours by Amy Dubois Barnett she stated that "Many women are paralyzed by self-doubt. We tend to be conservative and apprehensive when it comes to new experiences. We are too insecure to push ourselves out of our comfort zones." I began to turn her conviction over in my mind, and the question popped up in my head, "Are you a wallflower or a centerpiece?"

In order to be able to answer that we need to first clarify the distinguishing features of each one.

Definition of a wallflower according to the urban dictionary:

A type of loner. Seemingly timid individuals who no-one really knows. Often some of the most interesting people if one actually talks to them.

Someone, who sees everything, knows everything, but does not say a word. They cannot handle having someone pay attention to them even though they crave it as much as everyone else. Wallflowers fade into the background.

Definition of a centerpiece according to Macquarie Dictionary:

A centerpiece is the most important item of a display, usually of a table setting. A centerpiece also refers to any central or important object in a collection of items.

Whose responsibility is it to bring to light the beauty of a flower that is hidden amidst a thousand replicas? We each become the interior decorators of our own unique lives. We have the power to choose where we will stand in this world either front and center or in the wings of obscurity. Michael Jackson told us, "Life ain't so bad at all if you live it off the wall."

It is imperative that you come to an acute awareness of how important and valuable you are to society. **Someone is waiting to behold the rare qualities that only you possess.** I dare you to rest confidently as a centerpiece of distinction who is destined to attract the attention of countless admirers. You were created to change the atmosphere, what are you going to do?

The woman I am today would not be as internally strong without the iron walls of opposition standing in my way. Every experience taught me to trust at deeper levels than I ever imagined possible.

"The hardest step she ever took was to blindly trust in who she was."

–Atticus

Now go out in the world and beam wider than you could ever dream. Shine until every frown is turned upside down.

C.P.I.L.L. Confidence Prescription for Progress

Crownfirmation: I will unapologetically light up every room I walk into. I am fearfully and exquisitely made by the hands of God. All my perceived imperfections are made flawless in the ocean of His love.

Pause to Ponder: What I love most about who I have become and who I am becoming is?

I Celebrate:

Leadership Lesson Learned:

Lifestyle Elevation: Every Day I Will,

Day 19

Depression

A mood disorder marked especially by sadness, anger, inactivity, difficulty in thinking and concentration, suicidal tendencies, significant increase or decrease in appetite and time spent sleeping, feelings of dejection and hopelessness.

Dear Queen,

During the darkest days and nights allow your passion to be a guiding light to bring you out on the winning side. When you decide to no longer allow excuses to rob you of your deep-seated dreams, the rich rewards of change will fill your heart with unceasing ecstasy. **Embracing the courage to change infuses you with the ability to do something that terrifies you.** It will enable you to face unbearable pain and grant you strength to transcend troubles barricaded in your way. The exquisiteness of change is forever seen, the instant you lovingly admire in a mirror's gaze the person you have become versus the empty shell of one who is long gone.

There have been instances where my greatness was discarded. I was determined to muster every ounce of passion and resolve to be relentless in the midst of adversity. After I shed a few tears, I decided to pick up my pen and write: 'The diamonds of destiny are often discovered in the depths of despair. It does not matter if others can perceive the vast potential you possess. The question is, are you aware of the resplendent potency buried deep within? The opinion of doubters, naysayers, and unbelievers is irrelevant, insignificant and inconsequential in lieu of your divine purpose'. In the voice of Life Coach Valerie Burton, "I refuse to stare at closed doors."

At some point in our lives, we will all experience some type of unpleasant situation that leaves our hearts shattered and scattered in various directions. This state of mind should not be a normal way of living. If it is, the medical community classifies it as depression.

Recently, I discovered a definition of depression that vividly expresses what is happening emotionally beneath the surface. A depression is an area that is sunk below its surrounding. It is that moment when you feel weighted down by the storms of life, void of inner strength to rise above the tumultuous winds and waves that continuously crash against you.

What makes depression difficult to recognize is that it can be easily masked because it is more so an internal disposition rather than external. This is one of the reasons the world was shocked when comedian Robin Williams committed suicide. It is important for any individual to remain consciously aware of how they are feeling on a regular basis.

Here are a few self-reflection questions to ask yourself in order to determine whether or not you are in mental combat with depression:

Have you noticed a sudden negative mood swing in your attitude?

In the past few months did you encounter a minor or major disappointment?

Are you currently having any financial or relational challenges?

If you answered yes to at least two of the questions above, resolve to focus on solutions to alter feelings of lowliness and ascend above any perceived misfortune.

First, tell a confidant or companion how you are feeling. An unhealthy way to deal with your issues is to bottle them up so tightly until they explode unexpectedly leaving you emotionally out of control.

Second, if you have been in this slump for more than three months seek professional help to assist you in navigating through the process of stabilizing your emotional frame of mind.

Lastly, remove any unnecessary activities and keep your commitments to a minimum in order to carve out space and time to nurture your spirit.

Do you want to know the real reason you are battling frustration? As a creative being deep down within, you have vast amounts of potential that have yet to be excavated and explored.

It is a dangerous thing to fall into the depths of self-pity over problems, pain, and pressures that life throws your way. Instead of wasting precious energy on what is not working, create a laser focus on the bright future shining in front of you.

When we give in to frustration, the feeling of being upset or annoyed, especially due to an inability to change or achieve something we willfully relinquish our internal power to temporal circumstances.

The key to thriving amidst turmoil is learning how to master your emotions under extreme duress. How often do you rehearse self-defeating statements in your mind as a result of being annoyed in spirit? We inadvertently lose valuable time resuscitating negative thoughts that should remain dead and buried.

Listen closely to what you are saying in moments of mayhem.

"I've had enough."

"Can I get a break?"

"I'm tired of having to tired of fight for everything."

"I can't ever seem to get ahead."

"Who will hire me without a high school diploma?"

"If it's not one thing it's another."

In order to win the battle and constant war raging in your head, learn to re-direct your attention at the onset of unconstructive thinking.

- Focus on the Future. Believe the best is yet to be.

- Free yourself from unrealistic expectations. Greatness takes time.

- Fight and not faint. Quitting is not an option.

- Find your center. Delight in all that brings you sweet serenity.

Always remember, there is victory in the valley, rise to the occasion and slay every giant standing in your way.

You were designed to progress, not digress. Keep focused on moving fervently forward, not silly sideways, going in clueless circles or blundering backward. I challenge you to march upward and onward until victory is secured.

Listen quietly to sound of hope echoing in your soul, "There is a jungle of jubilant joy taking over. In the marrow of my bones, flows a rushing river no earthly force can control. I dance to the rhythm of my own drumbeat, who would dare protest me? Give me glitter, give me gold, give me freedom, give me fire, give me brand-new wings to soar higher. The wall of opposition may erect, but I will tear it down brick by brick."

On today, take a deep breath and:

Trust that the timing is perfect.

Trust that your voice holds mountain-moving power.

Trust that hearts will be ignited by your white fire passion.

Trust that your galactic vision will come to pass.

Trust that your unique life is full of purpose.

Trust that your strength will prevail.

Trust that you can ascend from poverty to prominence.

Trust that your future is brimming with limitless possibilities.

Simply put: trust, tread, and triumph.

C.P.I.L.L. Confidence Prescription for Progress

Crownfirmation: I trust in the truth and stand firmly upon what I know. My inner resolve is unbreakable, and my vision is unshakeable. I eat from the mountains of empowerment not the valley of my emotions.

Pause to Ponder: When do you feel it is most difficult to keep your spirits high and trust that everything will work out in your favor? Why do you think this is an arduous undertaking for you?

I Celebrate:

Leadership Lesson Learned:

Lifestyle Elevation: Every Day I Will,

Day 20

Confidence

The feeling or belief that one can rely on someone or something, the quality or state of being certain or a state of mind or a manner marked by easy coolness and freedom from uncertainty.

Dear Queen,

It can be unearthing to experience perplexing and fluctuating circumstances that rattle your confidence. Unplanned misfortunes are surprising opportunities to become acquainted with new might hidden from our site. For the first half of my life, I was as quiet as a mouse and was too afraid to speak out.

Confidence is built by courageously demonstrating a belief in yourself. Every time you take action despite fear, confidence increases. Every time you start again after a setback, confidence increases. Every time you pursue a goal and succeed, confidence increases. Every time you release unworthiness, confidence increases. Every time you walk away from toxic environments or influences, confidence increases. In this sacred space, shed who you once were, shed who society labeled you to be, shed the mask of pretention, shed every false belief. Robe yourself in radiance, in resilience, in royalty.

Our confidence is often eroded by fear. This inhibition shows up in multiple ways. We fear the opinion of others, we fear success, we fear failure. We fear challenge, we fear lack, we fear our brilliance. We fear making mistakes, we fear standing out, we fear truth, we fear lies. We fear being ostracized, and we fear the power we see as we look into our own beautiful eyes. As a result, we fail to give ourselves permission to live confidently and hold on to passé perceptions that keep us standing still on the shore of safety. **There comes a time that greatness will provoke you to step out of the boat of limitation and walk on the water of your faith.** I know what it's like to be a prisoner of pain, a slave of condemnation, a hostage of shame, and a captive of confusion. We must embrace not just the pretty parts of truth but the ugly parts as well. This is where an unshakeable confidence thrives and resides.

It's not complicated.

All you must do is:

- Un-complicate your life.

- Release people, places and activities that deplete your energy.

- Attune your ears to the still voice within.

- Rest in the power of unshakeable confidence.

- Listen, you know precisely what step to take next.

- Shift your internal disposition from misery to magnificence.

- You are stronger than your struggle.

- Arise from your bed of defeat and walk victoriously.

- Peel off the layers of yesterday that no longer agree with who you are destined to be.

- Allow the absolute truth to be your compass to be your gentle guide.

In the sentiment of Lisa Nichols, live as if you have "Nothing to prove. Nothing to hide. Nothing to protect. Nothing to defend."

When insecurities begin to whisper in your ear let confidence speak back to you.

How can I begin to express myself fully?

DARE.

Where do I find the strength to carry on after losing it all?

INSIDE.

When will I know it's the right time to move forward?

TRUST.

Why does life appear to be overwhelmingly complex?

PERSPECTIVE.

Who am I destined to be?

DECIDE.

C.P.I.L.L. Confidence Prescription for Progress

Crownfirmation: I will remain confident in the midst of chaos and confusion. I embrace the deepest parts of me, the darkest parts of me, the daring parts of me, the dynamic parts of me and the delightful parts of me.

Pause to Ponder: There are soul-crushing moments when we find our confidence dwindling to nothing. What situation are you currently experiencing that makes you sit down instead of standing up? Who do you have confidence in and what gives you confidence?

I Celebrate:

Leadership Lesson Learned:

Lifestyle Elevation: Every Day I Will,

Limitless

Without end, limit, or boundary.

Dear Queen,

What is on the billboard of your mind? Every week in my interactions with women I've discovered we each have the tendency to magnify our weaknesses and diminish our strengths. As you seek to evolve into the highest version of yourself, develop the practice of amplifying your advantages and silencing your shortcomings. **No matter where you are or where you have been, you are destined to win.**

Can you conceive a realm void of restrictions where you are granted the autonomy to be as inventive as your mind would permit you to be? The real prison is often behind the bars of narrow thinking. Consider why you constrain your potential with the chains of apprehension. In my experience what I have found to be the problem is wanting to protect my ego from the embarrassment of falling.

I distinctly recall the time after undergoing the daunting disappointment of losing my first building space as an entrepreneur. To return to the eight to five job I walked away from was emotionally crushing. I cried for three days because I knew how unhappy I was in my former place of employment. I was well acquainted in how constricting it felt to walk through those doors each day.

The appeal to live an expansive life increased day by day swelled from a whisper to a roar. No matter how much I wanted to ignore the sound of freedom knocking at the doors of my heart, it would not relent until I surrendered once again. To dare to live without limits will demand countless acts of courage; it will push you beyond your natural capacity; it will test your internal fortitude and mental resolve. The rewards of saying yes to limitlessness is indescribable. You sit in the pilot's seat of destiny with the freedom of choice to go wherever you desire to go. The question is what will you think of next? Your imagination is a blank canvas that awaits the expression of your creativity.

The challenges of life often immobilize us mentally, emotionally and physically, unless we determine within ourselves not to permit anything to keep us from achieving our goals. **If confusion is a jungle, then clarity is perceiving a bird's nest of opportunity in the midst of it.** The number one hindrance to destiny fulfillment is misguided loyalty. Your social experiences have skewed your perspective causing you to be loyal to your fears, loyal to your pain, loyal to your insecurities, loyal to your shame, loyal to your past, loyal to your non-progressive circle, loyal to your labels, loyal to your poverty, loyal to your disadvantages and loyal to your failures. **You possess the power to turn your life around today. It can happen in an instant**. The moment you decide to live without limits you become limitless. It's time to be loyal to God, loyal to your greatness, loyal to your legacy, loyal to your passion, loyal to your purpose, loyal to your vision, loyal to your family, loyal to your dreams, loyal to your mission and loyal to your destiny.

"The opportunity of a lifetime must be seized in the lifetime of the opportunity."

–Leonard Ravenhill

There is a Peruvian Proverb which says, "Little by little, one goes far." This is how you start stretching your beliefs far and wide—by acting on a single thought at a time. When I seek to venture into discovering what I am capable of I write out twenty-five losses that will occur if I fail to push the boundaries of belief. **What are all the internal and external rewards you will miss out on?** Any time that I am treading through a valley of dismay I say to myself, "When in doubt, be bold and be brave."

I fight continually to be healthy, and in December 2017 I found myself in the emergency room after finding out I had high blood pressure during a routine dental cleaning. The emergency room doctor wanted to give me to start taking prescriptions immediately. He only presented one option for healing and never inquired if I wanted to take a more natural approach.

The nurse who was checking me out came close to me and spoke silently in my ear. "I don't know why they prescribed this medicine, but during our board of nurses meeting we were told that women who take it begin to suffer from kidney problems." She showed me the loss that would incur if I didn't choose to look for an alternative solution for my health issue.

I chose to become my own wellness advocate and began to research extensively on how to decrease my blood pressure naturally. There was extensive research that proved if you change your diet, monitor stress levels and exercise moderately, hypertension could be eradicated from your life. The art of problem-solving is concealed in the paintbrush strokes of opportunities, solutions, and probabilities.

The skies open wide for the imagination that dares to scale the mountains of limitation. **Even the tiniest star is within reach when you have the goad to believe.** Search beyond the rope of restrictions and embark on an exciting quest exploring the frontier of boundlessness.

C.P.I.L.L. Confidence Prescription for Progress

Crownfirmation: There is no limitation that can keep me from my destiny. Who I am today cannot hold a candle to who I shall become tomorrow.

Pause to Ponder: It is often the details surrounding how we will accomplish a goal that prevents us from moving forward. If you had the perfect set of circumstances what is the first thing that you would do? Start there. Attack and don't look back.

I Celebrate:

Leadership Lesson Learned:

Lifestyle Elevation: Every Day I Will,

Day 22

Purpose

What one intends to accomplish and attain or the feeling of being determined to achieve something great.

Dear Queen,

The discovery of purpose may be revealed at multiple points in one's life. I believe the beginning awareness of who I was created to be awakened in October of 1996. This was my senior year in college, and I was tired of treading through the dungeon of disappointment, discouragement, and defeat. I had no sense of self-worth, direction or destiny. On a Friday night, while under the influence of alcohol, I came face to face with the misery of my mistakes. Standing in silence at the crossroad of change, I turned my back on the pit of pain and pivoted into a life of purpose.

For many years, I lived beneath my potential, a typical underachiever doing just enough to get by. I was the oddball. The class clown. The misfit. All in one. In middle school, I received a low score on one of the standardized tests that determines your academic placement when transitioning to high school. I failed and was assigned to basic level classes. Internally, it didn't sit well with me because I never experienced being in an environment where I was considered less than brilliant. The classes were not challenging, and I approached my guidance counselor to see if she would allow me to enter regular level classes. She agreed to it only if I maintained my grades. I will never forget Ms. Baldia because she deposited a seed of hope for the possibility of going to college. It would mean taking geometry and algebra II simultaneously when math was an arduous subject for me. I barely passed by the skin of my teeth, but I am proud to say that as a result, I was able to meet the criteria for incoming freshmen at Florida State University. I would be one of the first in my family to attend college. It was the beginning of winning.

As a college student, I still had to work through a very negative outlook on life. I had to work through bad habits and character traits. I was not very responsible, to say the least. I can remember ending up in the Dean's office for fighting. After going through the motions for four years, I selected criminology as my major, which was known to be an easy degree to ensure I graduated. My professor who was the only African American who inspired me to speak in class. He stated, **"Nothing pains some people more than having to think,"** a quote by none other than my hero Dr. Martin Luther King, Jr.

I was always sitting in the back of the class, blending in and too afraid to use my voice. Dr. Billy Close asked a question, and for the first time, I spoke. My answer was wrong, but on that day something powerful took place. I was liberated from the fear of sharing what was on my mind. I sat at my desk as tears fell from my eyes. If freedom to unleash what was inside of me was all I obtained from my college education, it was well worth the effort. I had to finish what I started and graduate because my mom sacrificed more than I could ever repay. I wanted to become a woman she could be proud of. She has been the wind beneath my wings, and her love is the underlying inspiration in all I place my hands to.

Your purpose must be bigger than material possessions and vain deceit. It must be an unquenchable fire blazing in the crevices of your entire being. If you are struggling with your self-worth, I am here to remind you that you're still a diamond. It's time for you to be liberated from the pain of your past if you plan to enjoy the pleasure of God's most precious promises.

Every person on this planet is encountering private battles that can be emotionally baffling. Whether big or small you have the power to overcome it all. The number one reason most people refuse to change is, they've become addicted to remaining the same. If you are unhappy with life, write a new chapter and see where your imagination leads you.

How can you know what your purpose is beyond a shadow of a doubt? If anyone were to enter your presence what will you guarantee they would experience every single time? If they came to me it would be, inspiration guaranteed. Bridget Borgogna richly explained it this way: "Your life's purpose is having an understanding of your own unique talents, your destiny, your specific role in life. Your vision taps into your energy and drive, your calling, a feeling of what you're supposed to be doing, your purpose. When you can see in your mind's eye your potential, you realize it and do something about it. I dare you to own what you'd like to do, what you'd like to have, and what you'd like to feel. It is in that space when your purpose will flourish.

118

I've had incalculable occasions that have plunged me into the wild wild west of entrepreneurship. The first major one was December 6, 1999, after being laid off at the homeless shelter. I was an information and referral counselor to homeless women. My heart would be torn at the emotional torture I witnessed these women experience. There were many days where I walked upstairs to one of the private office rooms to cry my eyes out. When I was terminated without notice, all my eggs were in one basket. I told myself that I would never again permit one organization to dictate my financial solvency.

Women frequently say, "I don't have start-up capital." Honey, that was the story of my life. What I teach them to focus on is their internal resources. I learned how to be creative in crisis. After twenty years of trial and error, what remains consistent is my persistence. This is my superpower. I have gone through hell and high water, and I don't look like the adversity I've had to endure.

In my mind, I am invincible, which means too powerful to defeat and victorious over everything. I used to waste so much time wondering if I should take the leap from my eight to five or stay. I took the leap, fell flat on my face and went back to the drawing board. There is no perfect path to your dreams; it is full of twists and turns. If you launch out into the deep, I can assure you of this; there will never be a dull moment. I have sat in that small cubicle feeling like a caged lioness, and yes, it's safe to a certain degree, but it can also be the suffocating death of your destiny. My health suffered many years in a toxic corporate work environment where I often broke out in hives from the internal anxiety. I now play by the rules that I write. I live according to my values. I am happier and healthier because I dared to step into my power.

As women in the 21st century, we commit to more projects, events, and soirees than we have reasonable time for. It is important to establish boundaries and value-driven priorities. Yes, you can do anything but leading lady you don't have to participate in everything. Secondly, the power to be is in the courage to do. Although you may feel powerless, the moment you decide to rise above your circumstance you become a powerful force to be reckoned with. It essentially boils down to a decision to think and act differently. Thirdly, purpose is embedded in the center of our passion. When you awaken to that which dwells on your mind day and night, the idea that you are willing to pursue for the rest of your life you are on the brink of colliding with dynamite. **In the crevice of your purpose is where power resides.** When you become cognizant of your divine power and walk boldly in purpose, you can tap into limitless potential. Wherever you are in your journey remember your wings already exist, they are simply waiting for you to take flight.

C.P.I.L.L. Confidence Prescription for Progress

Crownfirmation: My purpose is greater than the pain I am feeling. Calculated advancements produce clever attainments. I am surrounded by futurists who focus on my destiny not my history. I am free to lead and succeed.

Pause to Ponder: What is your divine purpose?

I Celebrate:

Leadership Lesson Learned:

Lifestyle Elevation: Every Day I Will,

Day 23

Release

To set free from restraint, confinement, or servitude, to relieve from something that confines, burdens, or oppresses, it implies a permanent removal from whatever binds, confines, entangles, implies the liberation or emancipation of a person from subjection or domination.

Dear Queen,

It does not matter how long you attempt to ignore the call of freedom. The piercing sound will ring louder and louder. This is the soul's cry and distinctively designed to alarm only you. A million people can be crowded around and never hear the cymbals of liberation resounding in your ears. The greatest gift I have ever given to myself is permission to let go.

Tony Schwartz said we should, "let go of certainty. The opposite isn't uncertainty. It's openness, curiosity and a willingness to embrace paradox, rather than choose sides. The ultimate challenge is to accept ourselves as we are, but never stop trying to learn and grow."

As an entrepreneur who walks on the water of my faith day after day, **I practice the art of letting go on a continual basis.** I must let go of how I think my day should flow. I must let go of who I perceive holds the key to my next opportunity. I must let go of disappointments and missed deadlines. I must let go of offense and bruised feelings. I must let go of pride and self-reliance. I must let go of yesterday's triumphant victories. I must let go of who I thought I was. I must let go of thoughts that lead to future failure. I must let go of the desire to be in complete control. I must let go of destiny restricting chains that I've worn like haute couture on my neck. It is in letting go that I am welcomed by a bouquet of miracles resting on my doorstep.

A woman who has been hurt deeply feels an instinctive need to protect herself. The iron partitions of disappointment become a barren stronghold that is dark and cold. She has lost the grace to be vulnerable, to shed a tear if necessary, to let down her hair and to laugh uncontrollably. Why are you clinging to dead weight? Uncuff yourself from lack, uncuff yourself from comparison, uncuff yourself from jealousy, uncuff yourself from toxic relationships, uncuff yourself from insecurities, uncuff yourself from dead-end jobs, uncuff yourself from the past, uncuff yourself from fear and uncuff yourself from anything holding you back.

We instinctively know when our season has changed, but the fear of the unknown keeps our feet chained. A young lady said to me, "It's too late for me to leave this job. I've been here too long. I know I just need to take the leap and jump." In response, I asked, "What are you afraid of?" **Think of all the wonderful escapades you could experience if you decided to design a fun and fearless life.** Understand this, the power to be does not require anyone handing you the key to liberty.

Have you pinpointed why it is so hard to let go of what has already transpired? Are you waiting for an apology from the person who violated your trust before you free yourself from the memory? Do you want restitution from your former employer for the time you've lost seeking to replace lost revenue? Are you angry with old friends for not extending the support you desired to obtain from them? Marianne Williamson powerfully said, **"Unforgiveness is like drinking poison yourself and waiting for the other person to die."** If you could step outside of the pain for a split-second and catch a glimpse of how you are deteriorating from the inside, would you continue to cling to yesterday's sorrow? The weightiest pain I have ever felt was during my adolescent years my dad was battling drug addiction. He would take my possessions and pawn them. I hated having to visit him in jail or the hospital after he had been in a fight with a local bad guy. I was angry from all the hurt he brought to our household and the unspoken pain my mother had to carry. I would sleep with a knife underneath my bed mulling beneath my breath saying, "I'm going to kill him." The burden of hatred was too much to bear, and one day I released it in order to be free.

Years later, he turned his life around, and I loved him deeper than I ever imagined possible. For eight years he fought bone cancer until his death on February 18, 2016. I watched a hard man became tender and compassionate. He never gave up on the possibility of beating his sickness. When I called to speak with him, I would ask, "How are you doing Daddy?" He would say, "I'm kicking, but not high." He was not going to allow anything to take his fight away. He released the need to be healthy and decided to make the most of every day given. If his attitude was different, we might have been robbed of a few more laughs, smiles and good times standing by his side.

Inhale deeply and speak these words of healing: "I choose to let go of every offense that has robbed me of joy, time, freedom, life, peace, progress, and opportunities. I know that it is effortlessly simple to release my heart of the hurt I will relinquish negative emotions as often as I need in order to live free. I will love without limits and bring hope to millions. Every morning I will wake up to a beautiful smile that reminds me how much sweeter life is when you stop, focus and exhale toxic beliefs. I am renewed, I am restored, and I am relieved. The clock is ticking. The door is open. The world is my oyster. The sky is my dwelling place. The ocean is my jacuzzi. I will not allow negative emotions to unsettle me."

There is always a choice; you can be bitter or be better. You can get mad or get motivated. You can choose to be resentful, or you can choose to release.

C.P.I.L.L. Confidence Prescription for Progress

Crownfirmation: I release all guilt, shame, and blame from past mistakes. I release unspoken anger towards anyone who may have offended me. I release all fear and anxiety concerning the future. I release the belief that there is a right and wrong way to express my authentic-self. I release every unhealthy habitual pattern that is blocking my progress. I release unproductive thoughts that no longer serve my limitless potential. I release unfruitful relationships that deplete my magnetic energy. I release every feeling of powerlessness. I release the need to be all things. I release my greatness to embrace the best of me.

Pause to Ponder: What top three negative experiences are you still holding on to? Write a goodbye letter to create closure on a chapter you will never live through again.

I Celebrate:

Leadership Lesson Learned:

Lifestyle Elevation: Every Day I Will,

Day 24

Prevail

To gain ascendancy through strength or to be effective.

Dear Queen,

Have you ever found yourself stuck in a rut of complacency, feeling trapped in the nook and crannies of your own mind? I have encountered almost every negative emotion known to woman and have learned it's the invisible things we cannot see that smothers us in a bed of defeat. The emotions themselves were not the issue. The main issue was being a slave to the whim of my emotions.

The word prevail means demonstrating the will to overcome and proving to the outside world that your resolve is more powerful than opposing forces. **How long will you pretend to be a tea light when you've been created to be a trailblazing torch?** Jonas Clark posed a question. "When trouble comes your way, will the mountain move your faith, or will your faith move the mountain?" Warrior queens are not moved by what they hear, nor influenced by what they feel but are fully persuaded and fueled by faith to believe. Whatever path you choose there will be mountains and valleys.

Evolving into a higher version of yourself will feel extremely uncomfortable and vulnerable to the zenith degree. It's called growth, change, transition, transformation, metamorphosis, and breakthrough.

127

The test of your metal will bring forth a shining new silver sword of strength that you did not know you possessed. There are going to be days when you question do you really have what it takes to be great? **Your obstinacy in the center of opposition will incite your own civil war to occupy and proceed forward.**

On today, grant yourself the freedom to create the life of your dreams as you step boldly into the power to prevail.

I give myself permission to prosper.

I give myself permission to weep and heal.

I give myself permission to love the insensitive.

I give myself permission to pursue galactic goals.

I give myself permission to walk in power, strength, and might.

I give myself permission to play by the rules I write, one letter at a time.

I give myself permission to shine bright like a diamond.

I give myself permission to travel the globe doing what I love the most.

I give myself permission to relax when I need to and roar when I must.

I give myself permission to breathe deeply from the wells of fulfillment.

I give myself permission to be extraordinary and dwell among generals of greatness.

I give myself permission to maximize my divine potential.

I give myself permission to live in freedom from fear.

I give myself permission to enjoy the beauty of life wherever I go.

I give myself permission to explore new ideas and experiment daily.

I give myself permission to stand out from the masses and powerfully exercise the profound wisdom that comes from inside.

I give myself permission to be abundantly blessed with the best of all things.

I give myself permission to sit in the lap of luxury.

I give myself permission to become all that I have been destined to be.

I give myself permission to live fully without reservation, hesitation, contemplation, trepidation, procrastination or explanation.

"They asked her, 'How did you free yourself?' She answered, 'By embracing my own power'."

–Yung Pueblo

C.P.I.L.L. Confidence Prescription for Progress

Crownfirmation: I liberate myself from the chains of fear, frustration, and failure.

Pause to Ponder: If anything was possible what would you aspire to achieve, what would you aspire to believe, what would you aspire to see, what would you aspire to receive?

I Celebrate:

Leadership Lesson Learned:

Lifestyle Elevation: Every Day I Will,

Reclaim

To recall from wrong or improper conduct, to rescue from an undesirable state;
to demand and regain the return possession of a thing.

Dear Queen,

You will step into your authentic-self the moment you discover what you do is merely an artistic expression of who you are.

Have you secretly desired to experience wild and outrageous success? What would having limitless possibilities at your fingertips mean to you? How many individuals would be impacted as a result of you living large and fully in charge? Are you cognizant of self-defeating thoughts that are attributing to a cycle of failure? Are you willing to implement significant change now in order to experience undeniable results later?

In the wise words of Socrates, "The unexamined life is not worth living." **Every circumstance you have encountered from childhood to present has shaped your thought patterns.** Whether you are aware or not, mindset greatly impacts your capacity to believe, receive and achieve.

We often spend a great deal of time making executive decisions that spring from an adolescent perspective. How do we prepare for uncommon success? The basic definition of prepare is to put in a proper state of mind or to make ready beforehand for a specific purpose, event or occasion. In order to become that which has never before existed, one must excavate old belief systems and import a new conceptual framework to build upon.

If you were to be frank and honest, what state does your mind currently reside in? Are you afraid of success? Do you feel undeserving of a better life? Why has success eluded you? How can you create a vastly different picture from the present moment? When you are alone, do you battle thoughts of frustration regarding the amount of energy you seem to expend with little reward for your efforts? When I am in an unmotivated state that is when I escalate my enduring faith and start speaking to my inner being. "This is not difficult to accomplish. You have done this before in less time. I am proud of you and how you live as a flaming light of inspiration. I need you to arouse yourself and grasp your goals. Plow deeper, push harder, pray longer until you claim your glitz, glam and gusto."

We all have the potential to inhabit an extraordinary existence if we dare to accept the notion that we have a divine right to abundant success and are committed to all that it will require of us in the transformational process. St. Francis of Assisi encouraged us to "start by doing what's necessary, then do what's possible and suddenly you're doing the impossible."

Let's look at five simple ways to prepare your mind to reclaim a new state of being:

1) **Become a sponge**, constantly soaking up new ideas to implement. Maximize every opportunity to learn from radio interviews, books, audio, and video programs, attending conferences, etc.

2) **Create synergistic relationships** with wealthy minded individuals who are successfully thriving in their personal and professional lives.

3) **Write down well-defined goals** and set out to accomplish short and long-term desires on a daily basis.

4) **Focus on expanding not shrinking.** Lead from a space of openness and attract abundance that alleviates lack.

5) **Act as if you already are and it already is.** Live from the future as you walk successfully in the moment.

The power is in your frequency, consistency, and intensity. Massive expansion demands massive execution. Laser focus is calling your name.

When you are rewiring your internal framework to go higher, it will not be without a fight. Think about the strength of water and how it can break a rock in half by constantly beating upon it day after day. This is how we shift our entire lives and break through the rocks of resistance. In the den of doubt remember, you are not called to comfort, you are called to be a champion.

Reclaim your strength. Reclaim your power. Reclaim your dignity. Reclaim your truth. Reclaim your peace. Reclaim your victory. Reclaim your health. Reclaim your prosperity. Reclaim your joy. Reclaim your resolve because there are greater works to be done.

C.P.I.L.L. Confidence Prescription for Progress

Crownfirmation: I boldly reclaim my right to live magnificently in the face of adversity. Today, I will take flight ascending mountainous heights to stake a claim on my divine birthright.

Pause to Ponder: What do you believe you need to fight for and reclaim today?

I Celebrate:

Leadership Lesson Learned:

Lifestyle Elevation: Every Day I Will,

Day 26

Identity

The distinguishing character or personality of an individual and the fact of being who a person is.

Dear Queen,

Mistaken identity generally comes as a result of mislabeling. Oprah stated, "What we are all actually seeking is the truest expression of ourselves." **Only you can determine what defines you**. Make a decision to not allow numbers to define you, futile opinions to define you, experiences to define you, disappointments to define you, socioeconomic status to define you, educational background to define you, popularity to define you, brand names to define you or anything outside of your brilliance to define you. You are unique and magnifique.

It's time to shift your life from 'un' to 'on', as the definition of un is not. The meaning of on indicates the continuation of movement or action. Are you wrestling with any of these confidence killers that blind you from seeing your true identity? Feeling undecided, unseen, unfitting, unfelt, unheard, unemployed, uncertain, unsatisfied, unpretty, unaccepted, unintelligent, unprepared, unprofitable, unworthy, unpopular, uninvited, undesirable, unsettled, untouchable or undeveloped.

136

At the very onset of these negative emotions, you must refuse to recoil and stand your ground. Boost your mood with these confidence builders, and tell your insecurities that you are uncommon, unbreakable, unconquerable, unforgettable, unprecedented, unwavering, unshakeable and unmovable.

In one of my vision books I have the words, 'I am who I make up'. **The most potent place to live from is having an awareness of who you are.** It has the same effect as knowledge. Once you know and understand a concept it belongs to you. The only way to lose it is if you forget it and it is impossible for a thief to steal this intangible gift.

Fortune favors the audacious.

"Do you want to know who you are? Don't ask, act. Action will define you."

–Thomas Jefferson

Are you in need of a promotion? Act as if it is already yours. Do you desire to start a business? Walk and talk like the boss. Do you want to marry the man of your dreams? Practice managing your home and your life as a wife with additional responsibilities would. Do you wish to wear attire that is two sizes smaller than where you currently are? Change your diet and exercise regularly until the weight falls off. You must be there before you get there. If you do not like the mirror image you see, take drastic action to transform your identity.

If you sink below a life less than you deserve you may never embrace the breeze of uninhibited enlightenment.

"Some birds are not meant to be caged, that's all. Their feathers are too bright, their songs too sweet and wild. So, you let them go, or when you open the cage to feed them, they somehow fly out past you. And the part of you that knows it was wrong to imprison them in the first place rejoices, but still, the place where you live is that much more drab and empty for their departure."

–Stephen King

If I could rewind the hands of time and converse with my younger self, I would tell her, "One day your voice will impact nations and inspire more women than you can ever dream of." I believe we all experience at some point in our lives the deafening silence that arises in a soul burdened by an untold story. **The greatness within us will remain agitated until we courageously unmute our voices and dare to boldly speak up.**

I was reading an Oprah Magazine one day at the hair salon. In her What I Know for Sure letters to the readers, she shared a statement one of her friends wrote to her during the 2012 battle for the Own Network. Oprah said, "I took the attacks personally. I was embarrassed to be perceived as struggling." Then on one emotionally low day in March, she received an email that read, 'You have omnipotence at your command and eternity at your disposal. Just thinking about you. Keep your head up. You're Oprah'. On those days that you forget who you are, remember your name carries great weight."

Our true identity has no correlation to our socioeconomic status, what we possess, who we know or where we reside. If you were to be stripped of everything you own all that would remain is your most authentic-self. We were born naked apart from any material appurtenances. The bitter taste of regret sometimes makes it more challenging to detach from the emotional stigma associated with a perceived setback.

Your former identity must be replaced with the attributes of excellence you seek to exemplify. **Take a twinkling second to say goodbye to your imperfections as you welcome in your next level.**

Dear Imperfections,

Thank you for the innumerable lessons. I understand now that true beauty comes in a plethora of shapes, sizes, and forms. You've revealed continuously that the best of me is often hidden beneath my fragile insecurities. You've taught me to have compassion for my emotional weaknesses. You've inspired me to cultivate inner strength in the midst of adversity. In every imperfection, I've discovered a life-giving radiant reflection. I marvel in the freedom of no longer being held hostage to outside opinions. Thank you for the gift of renewal in each jewel of truth. In my heart, I carry priceless treasures that allow me to shine whenever and wherever. In my eyes, pearls of power. In my nose, diamonds of determination. In my lips, emeralds of elegance. In my hands, rubies of resilience. In my arms, sapphires of steadfastness. In my hips, opals of opulence. In my legs, topaz of triumph. In my feet, ambers of ascension. In the crevice of my being, I house gems of greatness vivid enough for nations to perceive.

C.P.I.L.L. Confidence Prescription for Progress

Crownfirmation: I refuse to seek the consensus of the masses for my exodus. I refuse to cower when I hear the call to conquer. I refuse to prevent my imagination from running wild. I refuse to consult with critics who have yet to taste the sweet delicacy of winning. I refuse to play it safe by not reaching beyond what my faith believes and sees. My esteem is not influenced by outside invites, as my exceptionality is governed by divine insights. I am assured of who I am and where I am going.

Pause to Ponder: If you had an opportunity to have a private audience with all your insecurities what would you say to them?

I Celebrate:

Leadership Lesson Learned:

Lifestyle Elevation: Every Day I Will,

Day 27

Passion

Intense emotion compelling action. Passion applies to an emotion that is deeply stirring or ungovernable.

Dear Queen,

How do you know when you possess a pure passion for the things you do? One sign that passion is present is when you are engaged in something, and you do it because you cannot not do it. Once you determine what it is that you desire, you must be willing to make changes that will allow you to live out your passion. Staying connected to your passion is what sustains the inner strength to prod forward and overcome seemingly insurmountable obstacles.

"Let me fall if I must, the one I will become will catch me."

–Baal Shem Tov

Stephen Covey suggests in *7 Habits of Highly Effective People*, that passion derives from those things that naturally energize, excite, motivate and inspire you. I believe it would be grueling to walk away from true passion. I have been writing and creating stories since childhood. It is the air I breathe; the lifeline that feeds me continually. It is in every fiber of my being. I have a note on my desk that reads, 'Write until your eyes bleed'.

There are days that I feel myself drawing back in spirit, when the words on the computer are all jumbled up because I've researched too long and eyes exhausted from writing too much. Days when I've broken out in hives because my emotions are imbalanced, or I don't even know the date because I've been lost in creation. All of a sudden, I reminisce on a conversation held with my mother. She told me how my grandmother and great grandmother worked in the cotton fields from sunup to sundown earning a measly four dollars a week. I have the freedom to demolish the generational curse of poverty. What will I do with it? Use it or squander it? Being reminded of all the privileges I possess is the only match I need to ignite my fire to create a global revolution of dreamers to rise up and take their rightful place. Whitney Wolfe asked, **"Do you have a dream? Chase it down, jump over every single hurdle and run through fire and ice to get there."**

Passion is the sword of your strength to help you in the fight of your life. You will lose sleep to be with passion. You will run miles at a time to pursue passion. You will block out the entire world to be alone with passion. You will cry like a baby to hold your passion. You will lose sight of time just to have one more glimpse of passion. You will travel the world without a single dime to capture the essence of passion. You will plaster your office wall with seventeen vision boards just to feel the flames of passion. You will give your last breath to live eternally in the arms of passion.

"Going deep to find your passion is the ultimate adventure. Deep down inside, is not the scary place we think of when we imagine the deep sea, the depths of hell, or deep dark secrets. What lies between the surface and your center—those layers of fear, expectation, and conformity that bury who you really are is what makes the adventure seem frightening. We live with doubt about what we should do and who we should be because we are not guided to find those answers within us. Instead, external forces, our parents, our community, and our peers-often tell us what they want us to be and what they think we should do. We resist doing what we love because we are told what we are supposed to do instead. We create our own limitations."

–Lisa Hoth Dalton

Remember, you don't have to know everything to move forward. Say yes to yourself, yes to your dreams, yes to your future, yes to your greatness, yes to your potential, yes to your purpose, because yes changes everything. No-one can stop you but you. Howard Thurman said, "Don't ask yourself what the world needs. Ask yourself what makes you come alive, and go do that, because what the world needs is people who have come alive." Will you be a wet rag or a lit match?

C.P.I.L.L. Confidence Prescription for Progress

Crownfirmation: I possess new sight, new fight and will reach new heights. I will conduct my affairs through massive execution and cataclysmic paradigm shifts.

Pause to Ponder: What is the number one destiny driven activity you cannot go twenty-four hours without doing?

I Celebrate:

Leadership Lesson Learned:

Lifestyle Elevation: Every Day I Will,

Day 28

Fear

Anxious concerns filled with traces of timidity, trembling, and hesitation.

Dear Queen,

If you have breath in your body, you are ready. How often have you heard the little voice in your head saying, "You are not ready"? Almost every goal I seek to accomplish is missing a vital piece of the equation. Yet I refuse to allow it to imprison me with fear and stagnation. I remember one of my radio guests sharing mindset shifting advice. She said her mentor told her these words when she was wrestling with low confidence. "If you want to be the real deal then start acting like the real deal."

The problem is clear, you've been allowing the wrong voices to speak in your ears. There is safety in a multitude of wise counsel. How long will you consult with fear, whose primary objective is to confine your greatness? How long will you parley with pain, whose sole purpose is to keep you preoccupied with disdain? How long will you confabulate with envy, which is determined to blind you of your beauty, brilliance and bountiful blessings? How long will you ventilate with unworthiness, whose ancient plan is to ensure you never taste the sweet fruit nestled in the promise land? How long will you dialog with disappointment, whose number one focus is to impede you from reaching your divine destiny?

"The only real prison is fear, and the only real freedom is freedom from fear."

-Aung San Suu Kyi

The strength of a rose is hidden beneath its thorns. I confront internal fears every day with the unadulterated truth. Fear will always speak contrary to who you are and what you have been designed to do. Remembering my why gives me the courage to rise above the lies.

"Then I returned and considered all the oppression that is done under the sun: and look. The tears of the oppressed, but they have no comforter.

"On the side of their oppressors, there is power, but they have no comforter. Understand this, before elevation there must be confrontation."

–Ecclesiastes 4:1

There were mounds of potential deep within waiting to be unleashed yet I was a silent prisoner held captive by the fetters of my own fear. I will never forget the day I chose to step out of the boat of insecurity and walk on the water of courage.

It has been over twenty years since I conquered my fear of public speaking during my senior year in college. The one thing that I have learned about fear is that it is ever present and ready to challenge any forward movement. It is in that defining moment that you powerfully choose to ascend to greater heights and defy insurmountable odds.

You possess the power to dismantle fear and its useless advisory board. Move forward. Open access is waiting on you to exercise your sovereign authority.

The number one thing that immobilizes progress is fear. You need courage to speak and to soar, to live and to lead, to ask and to act, to connect and to change, to build and to bury, to grow and to grieve. Discover why you're here on earth and shake a tail feather, my dear.

As a leader called to impact others, there will always be someone searching for the light of truth, hope and direction that dwells inside you. Like a city set on a hill, you don't have the luxury to dwell in pity, you don't have the luxury to wait on perfect timing, you don't have the luxury of making excuses, you don't have the luxury of being mediocre and you don't have the luxury of living afraid. Those are costly amenities consumed by the lackadaisical.

The best way to get to the source of fear is by asking introspective questions. Do you fear failure? Have you experienced a tremendous delay in the fulfillment of your dreams? How did failure make you feel internally? Who do you lean on for help to weather the storms of life? What steps did you take to move beyond the crushing weight of hardship? Following the distressing situation did you view yourself as a failure or one who was strong enough to triumph and rise above the sting of struggle? These are vital questions to start the wheels of progress turning in a new direction.

It is inevitable that at some juncture in our lives we will come face to face with failure. As we aggressively shatter the shackles of fear surrounding the unknown or become acutely aware that what transpired in our past does not define us nor dictate the possibilities we are entitled to. How do you move beyond the crossroads of calamity? **Freedom is found, the instant you realize you were created with a purpose greater than any pain you will ever encounter.** It's time to face the bull head-on. Do not live in denial any longer.

Yes, it does matter that you haven't received a raise in five years. Yes, it does matter that he never returns your phone calls in a timely manner. Yes, it does matter that you give more than your friends reciprocate. Yes, it does matter that you've allowed yourself to become overweight. Yes, it does matter that you can't say no to drinking without restraint. Yes, it does matter that you find it hard to give thanks for at least one thing. There is a war going on for your destiny. How long will you remain apathetic about your life? Forward advancement does not yield without a fight. Look your bull in the eye and stare it down and take it by the horns until you bring victory home.

It is important that you re-define the meaning of failure to strip it of power. If you research the word, it simply means a temporary condition of not achieving the desired end. When things don't go as you plan, dust yourself off and try again.

"Freedom is the oxygen of the soul."

-Moshe Dayan

Recondition your mind to challenge what's challenging you because, what you feed, you will breed. A new course will require new courage.

Do that which makes you come alive inside.

Embrace that which wakes you up out of your sleep.

Pursue that which makes your heart beat with fiery passion.

Hunger for that which never satisfies the deepest parts of your soul.

Imagine that which inspires you to transform into the most magnificent version of yourself.

Live your life by design and not default.

Let's come into agreement that as you breathe and bulldoze through every obstacle standing in front of you, they will be removed. May every breath remind you to only seize what you believe is possible to achieve.

C.P.I.L.L. Confidence Prescription for Progress

Crownfirmation: I am transporting precious cargo that has the power to alter history. I will fear no-one but God. I possess faith-filled expectations to produce new life in every barren situation. I have grand expectations for unfathomable manifestations and infinite miracles that will leave me baffled by God's divine power. I am ready to step lively into a new dimension of ascension even in the face of bone-shaking apprehension. As I walk hand in hand with my faithful creator, I celebrate the strength to elevate, demonstrate logic-defying and unwavering faith to receive that which is beyond comprehension, unsearchable riches, notable acts of achievement and widespread global expansion.

Pause to Ponder: What fear is keeping your heart locked up inside? Can you identify the root cause of your fear/s?

Complete these sentences: I will overcome my fear by_____.

I can begin to love and accept by_____?

I Celebrate:

Leadership Lesson Learned:

Lifestyle Elevation: Every Day I Will,

Day 29

Energy

Positive spiritual force, or overwhelming power or great strength.

Dear Queen,

If life is breath, who are you? Are you deep, shallow, exhausted, frustrated, lively, full, excited or inconsistent? Every week, I speak with professional women who are mentally, physically and emotionally depleted. Many are overworked and underpaid. I have been on that side of the fence myself until I drew a line in the sand and made self-care a top priority.

Everything we see, hear or do can affect us positively or negatively. Perform a life energy audit and be honest about where you are and what changes need to be implemented.

1) **Vocation:** Where I work lights me up or wears me out.

2) **Relationships:** The people surrounding me empower me or drain me.

3) **Foods:** The foods I eat make me feel alive or sluggish inside.

4) **Environments:** The places I go inspire creativity or negativity.

5) **Media:** The visual communications I am exposed to nourish my mind or stimulate fear and anxiety.

6) **Clothing:** The attire that I select is tailor-made for my body or drapes off me in an unflattering manner.

One of my closest friends said to me, "I wish I had half of the energy you have." Every day I invest in my potential because I want to be a great human being who leaves a lasting legacy. I began to think, what am I doing differently that keeps me light on my feet?

Here are my top ten galactic goal slaying energy secrets:

1) **No private time, no public power.** As a true introvert who refuels through quiet times of reflection, my cup is running over by the time I come into the public space.

2) **I rarely watch television.** A treat is a Redbox video or going to the movies with my husband.

3) **I live in books and journals.** There is not a day that goes by where I am not feeding my mind via audio, written or visual content.

4) **As a content creator, I live in a receptive mode waiting for divine downloads.** This means I am very selective of who is in my personal space as I refuse to be a trash collector.

5) **The greater the goal, the more intense the focus.** If I believe it will take twenty-one days to accomplish a goal, typically it will consume eighty percent of my time.

6) **To eliminate the non-essential and get laser-focused,** I will often enter a fasting state where I eat once daily at 6:00 p.m. with two options: soup or smoothie.

7) **Place strict limitations** on casual phone conversations and social media activity.

8) **Physical exercise** five to six times a week to remain in a peak performance state.

9) **Have fun.** Life is meant to be lived to the fullest.

10) **In everything, give thanks**, the good, the bad, the happy and the sad.

"Start living now. Stop saving the good china for that special occasion. Stop withholding your love until that special person materializes. Every day you are alive is a special occasion. Every minute, every breath, is a gift from God."

–Mary Morrissey

On today, be confident in knowing you possess powerful potency to pursue your divine destiny.

C.P.I.L.L. Confidence Prescription for Progress

Crownfirmation: I am free from chains of limitation that once encircled my mind, body, and spirit. I am free from the need to please or be anything less than I was created to be. I am free from the shadows of struggle that seek to suffocate me. I am free from the wilderness of worry and iron walls of worthlessness. I am free from the confining cage of playing it safe. I am free to dream galactic dreams and live lavishly in the land of limitless possibilities. I am free to speak bodaciously. I am free to breathe. I am free… unapologetically free.

Pause to Ponder: My energy is often depleted immediately after:

The activities and people who ignite my dying flames are:

I Celebrate:

Leadership Lesson Learned:

Lifestyle Elevation: Every Day I Will,

Day 30

Opportunity

A set of circumstances that makes it possible to do something. A good chance for advancement or progress.

Dear Queen,

Powerful presence begins with acute self-awareness. It's time for you to step out of the shadows into the spotlight and shift from stuck to unstoppable. The moment you unmask your magnificence without reservation, brilliance welcomes you to the stage of greatness surrounded by a standing ovation.

I've been pondering something a dear friend said to me recently. "You are an opportunity magnet." As I sat at my desk early this morning, I began to reflect on what internal transformations took place prior to experiencing this magnetic life.

Celebrate the everyday every day. For many years, I battled depression behind closed walls, and because of my effervescent personality, it went unnoticed. **We must refuse to allow moments to impede our momentum.** I understand now that joy is more powerful than happiness. The latter is contingent upon what is happening whereas joy remains constant especially in the face of adversity. There is not one day that passes without me expressing gratitude for innumerable blessings received.

Become future focused. You will become an opportunity magnet the second you begin focusing more on your future rather than your fears, frustrations, failures, and flaws. **The fastest way to silence your inner critic is to fix your gaze on forward advancement.** It is one of the reasons I have seventeen vision boards and five vision books. What I expect is greater than what I currently see standing before me.

In my youth, I was notorious for putting off a task that needed to be accomplished. Perfectionism and procrastination will hinder progress, potential, and purpose more than any other self-sabotaging behavior. I live fully present in the moment as if this could be my last. When I was single, I remember imagining meeting the love of my life. I am always preparing for what is to come. I purchased a sophisticated blue dress for our first date. It sat in the closet for years until I decided not to put it on hold for a day that might have never come. I recorded my debut music CD in 2005 and wore that dress for the photo shoot. Last night, during my anniversary dinner, I was wearing a Calvin Klein blue dress that my husband purchased for me. Ironic huh?

Ascend from within. I say this all the time. You must ascend from within and choose to win. I raise my consciousness with affirmations. Daily, I wake and say, "It's a good day for a great day." I refuse to allow my emotions to control me. I declare over my day, "All I see is open doors before me. I have more opportunities at my disposal than I can receive." There was a time when I was at my lowest emotionally, financially and spiritually. Rock bottom. I had to muster up the last ounce of breath and on my knees still decree, "I fight, not faint." Your destiny is too precious to give up now.

Amaze yourself. The truth is, the opinions of others have been holding you back from living wild and free. I read once, **'If you want to be great, stop asking for permission'**. I want to encourage you to give yourself the green light and pursue your goals with gusto. Amaze yourself with bodacious courage to do things you would never do. Amaze yourself and travel the globe to the most exotic places. Amaze yourself and ask for the promotion you know you deserve. Amaze yourself and tear down the walls that are keeping you from experiencing unconditional love. Amaze yourself and finish the book that has been sitting on your desktop for three years. Amaze yourself and lose the thirty pounds you've been carrying around. Amaze yourself and start the business with the last one hundred dollars in your bank account. Amaze yourself right now, and before you know it everywhere you go, life will be nothing short of amazing.

I had to create my own opportunities because my life was without silver spoons, divine connections, brothers or sisters. It was hard work, goal setting, focus, prayer, and fasting. I have been graced to remain grounded through failure and success.

The ultimate freedom is refusing to allow achievements to go to my head or let disappointments poison my heart. Whenever you find yourself at that impossible junction, make a radical choice to roar, to soar and do more. Always remember, you possess the keys to success.

C.P.I.L.L. Confidence Prescription for Progress

Crownfirmation: I embody poise, peace, and power. I have a keen ability to quietly envision tomorrow's triumphs while treading through today's turmoil.

Pause to Ponder: What new opportunities will you open your mind and heart to pursue?

I Celebrate:

Leadership Lesson Learned:

Lifestyle Elevation: Every Day I Will,

Day 31

Womanhood

The state or condition of being an adult woman and no longer a girl.

Dear Queen,

When I was a little girl my shero was (and still is) Wonder Woman. After years of rebuilding myself, I had to learn how to be vulnerable. One evening, I shared with a close friend that I was feeling discouraged. She said to me, "I always think of you as the embodiment of motivation, and I forget that you have off days." I told her, **"Motivators need motivation too, and Wonder Woman is part human."**

The next morning, I found one of my vision board clippings on the floor in my prayer closet that said, 'Woman ABOVE all' and began to journal. 'I am woman above the fancy titles, accolades and credentials. I am woman above the success, awards and notoriety. I am woman above the pain, setbacks and disappointments. I am woman above the crisis, chaos and naysayers. I am woman above the inhibitions, internal anxieties and insecurities. I am woman above the mistakes, fiery trials and unrelenting adversity. I am woman above these things which have zero significance in eternity. I am woman above all the clamoring chatter that seeks to steal my peace. The truth of the matter is, I am woman above all and that gives me the power to simply be me.'

I've adopted the words of Jim Rohn as one of my personal mantras. "Ask not what I am getting, but what am I becoming?"

Consider at least fab five females to surround yourself with as you evolve as a woman:

1) **The encourager.** She will lift your spirits when you are battling moments of self-doubt. Dreams you've placed on the back burner will be brought to the forefront when you step into her presence.

2) **The straight shooter.** She is going to challenge you to be real with yourself, cut the excuses, provoke you to operate at a higher level of excellence, place a demand on your greatness and sharpen every dull place in your heart.

3) **The empath.** She is sensitive, feels your heart and knows why you do what you do. This woman is acquainted with you intimately and understands your past struggles, present concerns and future aspirations. You can trust her implicitly and have unwavering confidence in her loyalty. With her listening ear she will not judge you, only love you.

4) **The wild one.** Your life is full of responsibility, demand after demand. You are going to need a place where you can let your hair down and let the inner child run wild. Footloose and fancy-free. Endless hours pass by and all the laughter shared between you will do better than any medicine ever would.

5) **The oracle.** She has a direct connection to heaven and can hear God's heart concerning you. The bond established is not

earthly but eternal. It is unshakeable and unbreakable. In this intricate space of limitless creativity, multitasking and all things beautiful, a woman's world is spectacular. We give untiringly and often find ourselves tucked away in a quiet corner seeking a simple moment of solace. Men try to figure out how to keep pace, a feat they may never achieve. What makes this an amazing place to inhabit is the bond of strength that knits our hearts together through priceless experiences we share collectively.

Society has led us to believe that it is acceptable to criticize, scandalize and ostracize one another. There is nothing honorable about belittling someone in order to appear superior in stature. We are all cut from the same fabric of femininity and must learn how to celebrate our unique differences.

It is no secret that you are a mighty force to be reckoned with and yet it is the very thing that prevents you from connecting on a deeper level. Permit your shield of armor to fall completely to the ground as you take the chance to be vulnerable, delicate and tender as a budding rose.

How do you show up in your world as a woman? Have you taken time to assess the valuable qualities you possess? Are you rehearsing old wounds, mistakes, and disappointments of the past? Do you constantly second guess your best efforts or apologize incessantly? When was the last time tears filled your eyes with gratitude for every battle won? If you continue to dwell in the den of yesterday, how will you ever behold the fields of your future?

A woman's world was created to be as peaceful as a meadows stream, where heavy hearts may rest, and daring souls are unleashed to dream. A woman's world is a puzzle that even the most brilliant minds have yet to figure out. A woman's world is designed to cultivate champions of faith, not cowards of doubt. A woman's world must be governed by attentive detail and loving care. A woman's world is a magnificent mountain of possibilities in a tumultuous sea of insecurities. A woman's world is like no other and what an amazing work of art when we unite as one heart.

C.P.I.L.L. Confidence Prescription for Progress

Crownfirmation: I am not weak. I am a wonder and a woman. I choose to deal and not deny. I choose to heal and not hide. I choose to live and not die. I choose to rise and shine. From this day forward I am going to unfollow the rules. I am not okay with being just okay. I will challenge the status quo. I will speak up and speak out. There are many places I have yet to see, and I will get there by doing what's best for me. I will discover what I love and love what I discover.

Pause to Ponder: The aspects of my womanhood I am most proud of are:

I Celebrate:

Leadership and Life Lesson Learned:

Lifestyle Elevation: Every Day I Will,

Day 32

Pause

A temporary stop to linger for a time or to discontinue doing something for a short time before doing it again.

Dear Queen,

Do you ever feel guilty for taking the time to slow down and listen to the sound of your own breath? Societal pressure will make you believe that you are missing out on something if you decide to be still for a moment. **It is honorable to pause and ponder before you propel upward towards an awe-inspiring future.**

Years ago, in the course of my employment as a secretary, I experienced an emotional break down from exhaustion. I was burning the candle at both ends recording my debut music CD and writing my second book, *Follow Your Dreams*. If you were to ask me what straw broke my back, I could not tell you. All I remember was crying uncontrollably and being told by my supervisor to take the rest of the day off. I knew from that point on that I was going to have to deliberately extend myself an intermission on a regular basis.

Rewarding myself with mini-retreats has become a lifestyle. I believe there are millions of women addicted to the adrenaline rush of ambition. Statistics show that workaholics have a higher divorce rate, many people feel like their speeding through their day. If the company allows for vacation days, they are often unused. If a workaholic goes on vacation, the laptop is right there on the beach. You would think resting was a crime the way we seem to avoid it at all costs.

What I enjoy richly about the power of pausing is that it invites spaciousness into my mind. I can contemplate deeply about the delights and the dilemmas of life. In the hush of solitude, I can evaluate what adjustments need to be made in work, life, and play. We underestimate the vast benefits that result from nurturing ourselves. If your heart is aching, you can pour the oil of love on your open wound in this private place where internal needs are met. There will be times that you approach a crossroad. **In preparation for transition, you need a contingency plan, and in the tranquility of thought, you will know exactly which direction you should go.**

I give myself permission to pause from the cause. There is always a choice. I give myself permission to disconnect from the noise. I give myself permission to listen to the sound of my own voice. I give myself permission to dance in the winds of romance. I give myself permission to veer off course. There is always a choice. I give myself permission to breathe slow and deep. I give myself permission to feel pain and weep. I give myself permission to take soul-shaking risks. I give myself permission to hit and miss. I give myself permission to tear down walls until I see only waterfalls. I give myself permission to receive more than ever before. I give myself permission to be happy and continuously rejoice. There is always a choice. I give myself permission to be me, to live life abundantly.

A crowded mind has no room to think. Give yourself the freedom and space to create a magnificent masterpiece. Glow from the inside out and show this gloom filled world what pure radiance is all about. Where you live should not dictate how you live. Refuse to settle for anything less than freedom and abundance. Live generously but not to the point of insanity. To rest is to honor your body, spirit, and mind. To reflect is to revive your life.

May your mind be filled with peace, may your hands be draped in generosity, may your spirit be infused with strength, may your soul be overtaken with joy unspeakable, may your loins be girded with truth, may your eyes be guided with love and light, may your tongue be crowned with kindness, may your feet be swift to do good, may grace and mercy wash away your heavy burdens and may your deepest dreams come to pass every single day.

You were created to thrive not just survive. Can you see it? Can you hear it? That is the future beckoning you to reach higher than ever before. This is a defining moment; will you fearlessly choose to taste the sweet nectar of transformation?

I believe you already know this is an amazing adventure that you cannot afford to miss. I dare you to find out who you have not yet become and start glowing from the inside out.

C.P.I.L.L. Confidence Prescription for Progress

Crownfirmation: All that I desire is within arm's reach. I am ready to explore my limitlessness. I choose to remain poised for promotion while facing pain, pressures, and problems. From this day forward, I will advocate for my values as fervently as I fight for the rights of others. I will respect and uphold my personal boundaries without floundering. I will trust what my inner voice desires to say, it protects my best interests and will not lead me astray. I will be gentle with myself when I feel frail and unable to deal. I will slow down to breathe until I can hear my faintest heartbeat. I will love myself deeply and unapologetically. I will faithfully carve out sacred space to rejuvenate. I will remain calm in a crisis. When my world falls apart, I will remember I possess the gift of putting it back together. I am whole. I am well. I am woman.

Pause to Ponder: Why do you avoid creating sacred spaces for solitude? Can you identify the benefits of carving out time to replenish your spirit? How would you show up in the world if this was a normal part of your lifestyle? The moment I pause, I discover:

I Celebrate:

Leadership Lesson Learned:

Lifestyle Elevation: Every Day I Will,

Day 33

---~∾∾⁄⁄~---

Delight

A high degree of gratification or pleasure, extreme satisfaction and a strong feeling of happiness.

Dear Queen,

It's easy to fill our cup with delight when everything is going right, but it is a different story when the tides roll in. We miss the opportunity to delight in the simple things when we become preoccupied with the disappointments that leave our hearts heavy.

Mindfulness is the cornerstone of delight that guides us through the hardships of life. The definition of mindfulness is the ability to become aware of and focus on the present moment.

Think about your all that transpired in the last twenty-four hours. What were your first thoughts? What were your dominant emotions? Were you happy, sad, frustrated, overwhelmed or focused? Did you speak to anyone who negatively affected your energy? Who added the greatest joy to your day?

If we lack mindfulness, we deprive ourselves of the opportunity to delight in unexpected surprises. When I first married my husband, what I would hear him say more than anything was, "Sweetie, slow down." In my head, I was juggling two to three tasks at a time. I was a walking time bomb who constantly misplaced keys or locked them in the car. At some point, you get tired of your subjecting yourself to your own dysfunctional behavior. Practicing mindfulness has grounded me with vast emotional stability. Anything that we practice repetitively becomes a part of us, and that is why it is imperative to cultivate healthy habits. As I am more mindful, it allows me to find delight in hardships.

It is vital to ask the question, **"How do I want to live each day of my life?"** The truth is as long as we are here on earth, we will encounter good and bad. Deciding to delight in the laborious projects create meaningfulness in our work. My current perspective is that everything matters. How I treat my neighbors matters. How I care for my family matters. How timely I am to pay bills matters. How diligent I am in pursuing my goals matters. How I care for my body matters. How I lead as a business owner matters. How I conduct my affairs matters. How I use my voice matters. How I live my life matters.

Delight is a powerful shield that protects you from the hailstorms of discouragement. It will open your eyes to see through a colorful lens of hopefulness. During the worst season of pain, both financially and physically, delight became my lifeline. Every day I looked for a glimpse of good. I never stopped seeking for the bright side that always appears if stand at the right angle.

The simple pleasures often go unnoticed. From this day forward delight in all you see and do. Celebrate the significant impact you make in the lives of others.

The smile you shared, the clothes you donated, the parking space you gave up, the door you held open, the thank you card you wrote, the kind words you spoke to lift someone's spirit or simply lending a listening ear in the middle of a busy schedule. William Blake said, "The soul of sweet delight can never be defiled."

C.P.I.L.L. Confidence Prescription for Progress

Crownfirmation: My joy is not determined by what is transpiring outside of me but is dependent on my decision to delight in everyday things.

Pause to Ponder: What three to five activities bring you the most pleasure and on what days will you schedule them on your calendar to ensure that you are thriving not merely surviving?

I Celebrate:

Leadership Lesson Learned:

Lifestyle Elevation: Every Day I Will,

Day 34

Beyond

Out of the reach or sphere. Something that lies outside the scope of ordinary experience.

Dear Queen,

The future is here, the future is now, and the future is yours. If you don't learn how to demolish negative notions in your now, you will never be able to bask in the beauty of your next. The thoughts you magnify in your mind will manifest in every area of your life. Proceed passionately. Succeed steadily. Exceed extraordinarily.

For two years, I held the belief that my husband and I would pay off the mortgage on our home. We were intentional about exceeding our monthly payments, and it happened twelve years early. Supernatural debt cancellation goes beyond societal norms. In the words of Walt Disney, **"If you can dream it, you can do it."**

In 2007, when I traveled outside of the country, I barely had a hundred dollars to my name, but I believed that I could defy logic and go beyond my natural resources. The fundamental fact of existence is that this trust in God, this faith, is the firm foundation under everything that makes life worth living. It's our handle on what we can't see.

"The act of faith is what distinguished our ancestors and set them above the crowd."

—Hebrews 11:1-2 Message

If you are waiting for someone to co-sign your ideas, you might be standing alone for a long time. I want you to believe beyond having the support you think you need. When you are called to leadership, there is a specific assignment with your name on it to be completed, no matter what. We each have a giant that threatens our potential and will only fall by our hands. **You need courage to go beyond the silent whispers of doubt telling you that it is not going to work out.** You need tenacity to fight beyond the agonizing burn until the very end. You need patience to wait beyond what would seem to be a reasonable time to hold on.

I could not imagine going through life without the zeal to reach beyond what I see or play a losing hand as if it is a winning one. You do not have to accept what life throws at you if it is less than what you desire. You can have more. You can be more. You can do more. You can love more. It is only a few paces beyond where you are standing.

Sometimes, all it takes is one more phone call, one more email, one more sentence, one more question to embrace beyond. My husband and I broke up briefly during our dating phase. My heart ached beyond words, and I found myself crying often from missing him deeply. One day, a mutual friend asked him for my number to speak at her women's empowerment event. He called to relay the news, and we talked for hours picking up where we left off. We now say to each other one of our favorite quotes by Maya Angelou. "I am so glad you gave love one more try." It takes humility to go beyond misunderstandings. There is a breathtaking beauty that can only be captured after going beyond the norm.

You do not need to have it all figured out in order to move forward. If anyone lacks wisdom let him ask of God, who gives liberally to all. Go beyond perceived limitations. Go beyond the threshold of pain. Go beyond unwarranted and futile opinions of man. Go beyond the whispering doubts of what seems impossible. Go beyond the barriers. Go beyond the brink. Go beyond the best you believe you can be. We are not interested in the possibilities of defeat. They do not exist in the mind of a woman who dares to lead and succeed.

Believe your bodacious beliefs and ignore your disempowering doubts. Before you go to sleep, create a success script of how you desire every day to play out. Tell yourself, "I am expecting the best of best opportunities to knock on my door this week. I have more energy than I know what to do with. I have no need for an alarm clock because my passion wakes me up. I will meet and exceed my goals. I attract high caliber clients who value my wisdom, knowledge, and experience. I operate my business from a place of inner calm and unshakeable confidence. I receive an abundance of favor, wealth and prosperity because I give lavishly in service to all."

You are the executive producer of your life, and you possess the power to display an award-winning show day and night.

C.P.I.L.L. Confidence Prescription for Progress

Crownfirmation: I reach beyond the clouds of limitation into a galaxy of immense, incomprehensible. inexhaustible possibilities.

Pause to Ponder: What do you believe each life experience has been preparing you for? Do you notice the common thread in every encounter and the mission you are called to spearhead?

I Celebrate:

Leadership Lesson Learned:

Lifestyle Elevation: Every Day I Will,

Day 35

Priority

Superiority in rank, position, or privilege. Something given or meriting attention before competing alternatives. The condition of being more important than something or someone else and therefore coming or being dealt with first.

Dear Queen,

Is your life full, but shallow? Is it cherished, but dull from the same ole' routines? Do you sip at life or drink from it deeply?

Set your focus on what will receive your attention. To become a master of implementation and successful outcomes, it will require iron-clad intentionality. If you could place a price tag on your time and attention what would it be? In my astute opinion, I believe your awareness of how precious time is would prevent you from squandering mounds of minutes.

We often hear the word intentional, but what does it mean? A mental state that represents a commitment to carrying out an action that requires planning and forethought. In the medical field, it is the healing process of a wound. **Your goal, aim or purpose is intention. Intention is when you decide to take a specific action.**

Calculate how frequently your intentions are hijacked by distractions which are designed to divert your attention away from implementation that could catapult you into new dimensions of ascension. Why do you think sales and marketing is one of the most lucrative industries? They are trained to persuade to you change your focus from your priority to their profitability. If you are passive in thought, you will empty your bank account to finance someone else's agenda.

As women in the 21st century, there will always be a tug of war for our attention. **We must decide what is a priority and commit to giving the things that matter our time and focus.** Every day we will be presented with an opportunity to recommit to our highest priorities. As leading ladies, simplicity is overshadowed by our excessiveness. Hans Hoffman stated, "The ability to simplify means to eliminate the unnecessary so that the necessary may speak." What we permit, will continue to persist.

Priorities keep us from becoming overwhelmed by the big picture as we tackle the small pieces that lead to completion. The discipline of weightlifting has empowered me tremendously. My natural disposition and personality are fueled by spontaneity. I am a poster child for free spirits. When I set out to accomplish any task that seems daunting in nature, I shift into beast mode, and the butterfly wings are placed on the glass shelf.

In weightlifting, we attack our sets one rep at a time. If I thought about doing a thousand reps the moment, I walked through the gym doors, it might dissuade me from giving my all. Prioritizing is the ability to elevate your mind above the commotions that cloud your judgment. I elevated my eating habits one meal at a time. I elevated my circle one friendship at a time. I elevated my thinking one vision board at a time. I elevated my career one opportunity at a time. I elevated my appearance one article of clothing at a time.

Guard your goals and protect your priorities. First and foremost, they are to be catered to by you. We demonstrate the importance of our priorities through daily actions. If health is a top priority, the subsequent action would be exercising and consuming healthy foods. It is not what we say but what we do that that validate our values.

"Things which matter most must never be at the mercy of things which matter least."

–Johann Wolfgang von Goethe

C.P.I.L.L. Confidence Prescription for Progress

Crownfirmation: I will love myself lavishly and make self-care a top priority.

Pause to Ponder: Look at your day. Track how you are spending your time. Does it reflect what you value most in life? Your daily schedule is a snapshot of what you deem as important. Do you agree with your choices? If not, who's making them?

I Celebrate:

Leadership Lesson Learned:

Lifestyle Elevation: Every Day I Will,

Opulence

*Great wealth or luxuriousness. Lavish and visibly over the top living.
Abounding in resources.*

Dear Queen,

Opulence is your birthright. A special place of prominence is reserved
and ready for your arrival. Your current environment is not conducive
for the opulence that is on the horizon. Somewhere along the way you
lost sight of the priceless power you possessed inside and began to
lower your expectations.

**Every tangible manifestation begins with intangible
anticipations of what is possible.** I created my first vision book in
the year 2003 and filled with five-star preferred luxury hotels. As a
keynote speaker during my travels, my lodging accommodations are
exactly what I envisioned decades ago.

After extensive research of successful individuals, I have matured in
my understanding concerning wealth, abundance and prosperity. We
know that there are influential leaders who were born into success. The
ones who impress and inspire me are those who build an empire from
within that can withstand the tests of time. They did not have fine
china, but they laid out paper plates and plastic forks as if they were
being served at the Ritz Carlton.

Shortly after I received my termination from the Medical Day Spa, I was definitely not in the best financial position to travel and invest in a high-end coaching retreat. It was paramount that I surrounded myself with prosperous minded women who were winning. The entire experience was draped in extravagance from the restaurants to the hotel, to the Miami shopping venues and it was exactly what I needed to remind me of destiny. The more I positioned myself in places of prominence it became a manifested reality.

The opposite of opulence is an impoverished mindset which means to be deprived of strength, vitality and reduced to poverty. This is why it is crucial to tend to the garden of your beliefs and prune out any weeds that could possibly choke your prosperity.

As you think, you become the expression of your thoughts. Have you ever observed the conversation of those who are impoverished in spirit? It is filled with debasing words of despondency and woe is me. Opulence is rooted in optimism and oppression is entrenched in pessimism. The proper perspective holds the power to pierce through the prison walls of poverty-based thinking.

Arrange your calendar to accept invitations to the finest celebrations. Open your arms to receive a standing ovation. Lift your eyes to see a galaxy of prizes falling from the skies. Break out a colossal smile for the limousine ride because opulence travels in sophistication and style.

You deserve to have over the top adventures after all you've encountered. Plant your feet inside the golden gates of affluence and enjoy the benefits of preferential treatment.

Those who matter don't mind your shine and those who do have no say in the matter. Let a regal new you emerge; it's your turn to make a powerful comeback. Treat yourself lavishly and luxuriously, you reign as queen of chic in the city.

C.P.I.L.L. Confidence Prescription for Progress

Crownfirmation: I am a wealthy city standing under a rainfall of unyielding fortune and favor. I sit poised in the lap of luxury and rest peacefully in the arms of splendor. As I gaze through the windows of grandeur, I appreciate the grace to manifest an ocean of opulence, abundance, and extravagance. I have access to wealth, riches and opulence everywhere I go. I live in unlimited abundance. Prosperity within me. Prosperity around me. Prosperity over me. Prosperity through me. I am open and always ready to receive more prosperity. Every cell in my body is filled with vibrant energy.

Point to Ponder: Who do you have to become to walk in opulence and limitless abundance?

I Celebrate:

Leadership and Life Lesson Learned Today:

Lifestyle Elevation: Every Day I Will,

Day 37

Potential

Existing in possibility, capable of development into actuality, a power or quality that has not yet come forth but may emerge and develop. What does not yet have existence or effect but is likely soon to have. An ability or quality that can lead to success or excellence.

Dear Queen,

The journey towards greatness is one of the most intimate paths of self-discovery that you will embark upon. It is filled with rich rewards and the most strenuous challenges one can withstand. Our highest desires are patiently resting on the other side of our inhibitions.

When I was younger, dreaming was a way to escape from a volatile internal and external living environment. In simpler terms, I lived inside my head, and in the most crowded room, I mastered the art of being invisible. I began writing stories to escape the pain and journals were my mental health counselors. I would design clothes and dress up my Barbie dolls. Our childhood interests can indicate our future potential. As a creative adult, I ended up in beauty school, painting faces, teaching fashion modeling, competing in pageants, writing books and telling stories.

The number one hindrance to maximizing our potential is when we ignore the signs pointing to our pure genius. In college, the most logical subject to study would have been journalism, communication or music. I chose criminology an area of study that was eons away from my natural abilities.

The decision to live free from societal labels, cultural expectations, and self-imposed limitations can be clearly expressed by the words of Anais Nin. "The day came when the risk to remain tight in a bud was more painful than the risk it took to blossom." Exploring your potential is a continuous expedition into the unfamiliar. **Would you rather play it safe or discover every bead of brilliance hanging on the string of your potential?**

Awakening my passion for action unlocked the door to limitless possibilities beyond my wildest imagination. As a result of daring to pursue my dreams, I have had the pleasure of creating innovative products to inspire others to believe. This is the secret sauce to internal fulfillment when we become the embodiment of our innovative ideas.

I know individuals who change jobs every couple of years on the hunt for a more meaningful existence when all they have to do is surrender to the sweet nectar of their potential. **The only thing that can satisfy our soul is walking in the truth of who we were created to be.** We each possess unique qualities, raw material that has the power to transform into something spectacular.

A bakery starts out with ingredients that are separate until they all come together inside of a bowl. The baker places all the ingredients into a pan and places it inside a hot stove before waiting patiently for it to rise. Our talents are mixed with experience to create something spectacular for others to enjoy. First fire, then refining. This process removes anything that is not supposed to be a part of our potential. The icing on the cake is when we refuse to quit and come out glistening like silky smooth frosting.

The graveyard is full of wasted potential. You have the capacity to evolve from untapped to uncapped. Your distinction is revealed the instant you decide to crossover the bridge of mediocrity and greet your magnificence with a kiss, boldly declaring hello from the other side of a brand-new life.

C.P.I.L.L. Confidence Prescription for Progress

Crownfirmation: I possess the power to create new outcomes, new income and step onto new platforms to share generously the treasures of my heart with all who are seeking to discover what I have unearthed in the caverns of my soul.

Point to Ponder: What areas of your life have been shrinking back instead of stepping forward? How will you make yourself proud? What new habits can you instill in your daily routine? What new relationships or new business opportunities can you obtain? Whose life will you impact in a special way?

I Celebrate:

Leadership Lesson Learned:

Lifestyle Elevation: Every Day I Will,

Day 38

Expectation

Prospects of inheritance, a belief that something will happen or is likely to happen, a feeling about how successful something will be or the state of looking forward to or waiting for something to become a reality.

Dear Queen,

As you proceed by faith and not by sight, you will discover an oasis of life, soul-refreshing rivers in the midst of a barren desert. Smack dab out of nowhere these blessings shall accompany you wherever you go. To your left favor and to your right mind-blowing miracles. In front of you lie unexpected surprises and behind you are signs of wonder. This is the good life, and you've found your stride.

Allow your vision to give wings to your deepest dreams, to escort you to the most magnificent places you've ever seen and infuse courage to believe you can accomplish anything. Expectation is the hand grenade waiting to detonate and destroy any mountain of doubt that needs to be annihilated.

Imagine your life story on the big screen. What would the world see? Coming to a theatre near you, Relentless Pursuit. Based on the true accounts of a woman who refused to give up after fighting through sickness, abortion, date rape, divorce, miscarriages, rejection, struggle, addictions, poverty, low self-esteem, unemployment, depression, heartache, and loneliness. In the middle of misery, she remained true to her mission and message.

Ariana Dancu said it best. "She made broken look beautiful and strong look invincible. She walked with the universe on her shoulders and made it look like a pair of wings." Is this woman you? The one who refused to let the thrashing blows of failure decrease your expectation of a brighter day.

I completely understand the pounding desire to throw in the towel. The weight can be more than your natural mind can bear, and that is why it is the perfect time to enlarge your expectations. **You cannot afford to sit around moping about the people, places and things you've lost.** Expand your expectancy and fill your heart with an unshakable belief of what you can achieve.

Expectation is the breeding ground for miraculous manifestation. Expect prosperity. Expect liberty. Expect an open door. Expect more. Expect increase. Expect peace. Expect relief. Expect strength. Expect a yes. Expect the best. Expect the uncommon. Expect the unexpected. Expect the abundance of rain every single day. Shake the dust off disappointment. Rise in the light of your own fire and walk in the roaring torches that your spirit set ablaze. Sit enthroned on the seat of stability, security, and significance.

C.P.I.L.L. Confidence Prescription for Progress

Crownfirmation: I will courageously rise above the pressures of life, persist through the problems and prevail powerfully with all my might.

Pause to Ponder: My greatest expectation that I desire to experience a manifestation of is:

I Celebrate:

Leadership Lesson Learned:

Lifestyle Elevation: Every Day I Will,

Day 39

Stillness

The absence of movement, sound or disturbance.

Dear Queen,

I know firsthand how it feels to steer out of balance in your personal life as a result of the relentless pursuit of dreams. There is a distinct difference between being diligent in your efforts and being addicted to your work.

I know that I can do anything, but I do not have to do everything. Understanding this simple truth frees my entire being from false expectations and obliged participation. My heart depends on a watchful eye to choose what is best for the woman I will be in the near future. **Listen to your body. Listen to your mind. Listen to your soul. Listen to your spirit.** They speak a unique language that only you know. Healing is possible if you are willing to dive deep into places you've been too afraid to go. Be healed of every toxic relationship. Be healed of internal wounds. Be healed of your dependency on worthless substitutions of love. You don't need more; you need less. Yes, less clutter, fewer activities, less noise, less chaos distracting you from being whole. On today, bend your ear to hear crystal clear what your life has been dying to say.

Solitude is sacred. It is the time when I can navigate through the forest of my own life to listen to the still voice inside. I sit in the posture of being the student, naked and vulnerable with God about my purest truth. In this space, I am not the leader, the poet, the keynote speaker, the artist, the coach, the prophet, the prayer warrior, the wellness advocate, the wife, the best friend to the end, the comedian, the epitome of positivity and a great deal more. I am simply open to receive heaven's touch until I overflow with agape love. I realize we are all fighting the same battle: to silence the inner critic within.

Nikki Rowe stated, "In the stillness of solitude is where I place my chaos to rest and awaken my inner peace." Life as an entrepreneur can be fast paced. I often ask myself is it possible to live healthily and be a business owner? A resounding yes, but only if I refuse to neglect myself. There are constant demands on my time, deadlines to meet, brain power expended, energy drained, physical, emotional and mental strength pushed to its maximum capacity. One day after battling fatigue, I checked in with my spirit and asked, "What do you need?" I responded with, "Pampering." I called up a day spa and booked a massage. The gift I give myself is returning to center as often as I must. There will always be work to do from dawn until dusk.

Divine secrets are revealed the moment you decide to be still. Business builders often focus on the external structures, but I know countless entrepreneurs who are no longer self-employed because they cracked under pressure.

When my back is against the wall instead of falling apart, I dig deep within and search for the calm in the midst of the chaos. For many years I worked in highly toxic and dysfunctional environments. The chronic stress led to years of emotional eating and would often break out in hives from the internal anxiety. If I was going to thrive and not just survive radical changes would have to be made. Elizabeth Edwards eloquently expressed. "She stood in the storm, and when the wind did not blow her way, she adjusted her sails."

As a result of starting each new day with the intention of living well, loving well and leading well, imagine a calmer version of yourself without anxiety and overwhelm. In the words of Jim Rohn, **"When I change, everything changes."** Now is the time to pivot into new purpose, poise, and power. Awaken your inner glow and remain free to flow because you're worth it.

C.P.I.L.L. Confidence Prescription for Progress

Crownfirmation: I revel in the gift of divine health with open arms and slowly inhale and exhale my deepest breaths.

Pause to Ponder: How can you create stillness in your life? When and where do you need it the most?

I Celebrate:

Leadership Lesson Learned:

Lifestyle Elevation: Every Day I Will,

Invincible

Incapable of being conquered, overcome, or subdued.

Dear Queen,

The depth of your strength should come as no surprise or shock to you. I know it can be easy to lose sight of it when the ground is shifting beneath your feet. In your mind, you've been wondering if you have bitten off more than you can chew. Can you really see yourself nibbling on nothing instead of devouring mountainous dreams?

Your DNA is coded for invincibility, which makes it impossible for you to be defeated or conquered in combat. There is a war going on for your peace, your destiny, your hopes, your potential, your ideas, your family, your success and anything pertaining to your progress. If you were not a threat, you would not be experiencing a single attack or an attempt by invisible forces demanding you to step back.

Count the battle scars from every fight you've won, and then return to the front line. The end has not yet come. Now that you are in demand, you cannot fall apart like sand. There are soldiers waiting to move at your command. Put on your iron breastplate and refuse to faint under the scorching heat of adversity.

Our strength is often revealed long after we overcome the most intense battles against our resolve. The only way to get to the next level of advancement is to press through the current one. That is why it is imperative that you never stop unless it is to catch your breath or drink a refreshing glass of water. A warrior is not granted the laxity of taking extended sabbaticals. This is life, and it requires the best of you.

Ignore the negative reports, disregard the delays, and forget the failures as you tread into triumph. Keep focusing forward because victory has no room for cowards. Today is the day that you rise again. Today is the day that you inhale a fresh wind. Today is the day that you thrash your troubles. Today is the day that you pull down strongholds.

"Your success and happiness lie in you. Resolve to keep happy, and your joy and you shall form an invincible host against difficulties."

–Helen Keller

Be strong in your mind, be resolute in your determination, be rooted in your convictions, be brave in your speech, be strategic in your advancements and be unyielding in your aspirations. Remind yourself daily that you are powerful, strong, resilient, fierce, tough, unceasing, indestructible, secure, unwavering and committed to winning.

C.P.I.L.L. Confidence Prescription for Progress

Crownfirmation: Eyes wide open, with both feet on the ground I speak to my mountain and command it to stand down. I will defy every single odd stacked against me. I am not a victim. I am victorious. I am not helpless. I am heroic. I am not barren. I am blazing. I am not insufficient. I am infinite. I am not underestimated. I am unstoppable. I am not pitiful. I am powerful. I am not shallow. I am substantive. I am not miserable. I am masterful. I am not fearful. I am ferocious. I am not little. I am legendary.

Pause to Ponder: When was the last time you felt invincible? How did you astound yourself? What new bodacious goal is calling you to experience this feeling again?

I Celebrate:

Leadership Lesson Learned:

Lifestyle Elevation: Every Day I Will,

Day 41

Ease

The state of being comfortable: such as freedom from care, labor or difficulty, something that disquiets or makes burdens less intense.

Dear Queen,

I see you. I hear you. I feel you. I celebrate you. Years ago, I placed service over self, ambition over awareness and productivity over peace. There is a vast difference between being driven and being guided. The distinction is that your internal posture is one of calm rather than chaos. I would rather be a glow-getter than a go-getter. I have decided to choose people, places and things that make me come alive from the inside.

If you do not learn how to surrender to ease in your daily life, you may end up with dis-ease. The late Wayne Dyer stated, "Over 112 million people are on medication as a result of stress-related symptoms." He also noted that **there is no stress, only people with stress-filled thoughts**. How can we integrate self-care or wellness in our daily lives? The world is running 24/7, which means we must be proactive and learn how to put our internal clock on hold in order to reflect, refuel and renew.

As women, we often eat foods for comfort because it seems easier than emotionally dealing with the complexity of a crisis. One of the best ways to conquer your unnatural cravings is to embrace what is best for your entire physical being.

If you suffer from anxiety or depression, challenge yourself to avoid these items: fruit juices, carbonated drinks, white breads, coffee, alcohol or nutrition deficient processed foods. Reverse engineer your diet and select foods that create internal calm such as tuna or turkey, avocado, blueberries, almonds, walnuts, green tea, bone broth and oat bran. Adopt the wellness philosophy of Socrates to "let food be your medicine and medicine be your food."

It takes as much time to be carefree as it does to worry. We think that if we binge out on our favorite TV episodes, all our difficulties will disappear. We cannot discern the root cause of our unease if we continue to ignore how we feel. What can you specifically eliminate from your home, your refrigerator, your schedule or your life to decrease internal stress and un-complicate your day?

Sit down for a second and allow your mind to rest as you pay attention to every single breath. There is a more excellent way to lead, and that is from a place of tranquility. You can be productive and at ease, progressive and at ease, creative and at ease, successful and at ease, goal oriented and at ease. Executing your responsibilities from the mental space of ease will allow you to be proactive rather than reactive to external activities.

One afternoon, my husband walked into my home office and could not wrap his head around the seventeen vision boards on my wall. I know the persistent mind chatter that I have to wrestle every day.

Positive words of affirmation create a sense of ease when I need a reminder to be at peace. As I sit at my desk, I play instrumental music, light a scented candle, place my heating pad under my back and sip warm ginger tea with lemon. These small acts of kindness make the burden of business building feel lighter.

How do you fight the funk and heighten feelings of ease, especially on days when you would rather be an invisible dot on the wall? You fight it by spending quality time with the ones you love. By doing something fun that makes you laugh and enjoy the present moment. **Get fit, get moving and get your zest for life back.** Find someone to encourage and lift their spirits up. Focus on what matters most and express radical gratitude for the air you breathe. There is always something to be thankful for.

Before you seek a bouquet of flowers make certain your vase is full of water. Follow your bliss rather than become entangled with the chains of busyness. Permit your aura to be transformed into magnificence as you step into your Queenfidence.

C.P.I.L.L. Confidence Prescription for Progress

Crownfirmation: I flow with ease, walk with elegant grace and speak with enchanting flair.

Pause to Ponder: The area of my life that I seek to experience more ease and grace in, is:

I Celebrate:

Leadership Lesson Learned:

Lifestyle Elevation: Every Day I Will,

Day 42

Strength

The power to resist force the quality or property of a person or thing that makes possible the exertion of force or the withstanding of strain, pressure, or attack. The ability to resist being moved or broken by force. The quality that allows someone to deal with problems in a determined and effective way.

Dear Queen,

What makes you question the strength you possess? Krysten Ritter said, "Strong people, meditate. Strong people stay present. Strong people laugh at their fears. Strong people find the good in bad experiences. Strong people, embrace being unique. Strong people humbly apologize. Strong people, pay it forward."

I needed a shero, and that is who I became. Living on the other side of pain is pure oxygen, and it allows me to see the strength I've gained. Strength is allowing myself the freedom to be vulnerable, to love deeply, to go the distance, to support the helpless and to tame my powerful tongue when it desires to be flippant.

Strength is the grace to share the gift of good news while staring down a heap of negativity. Strength is refusing to permit failure to dictate your future. **Strength is challenging status quo mindsets even if you must tread alone in the trenches.** Strength is making peace with the past and reaching for goals beyond your grasp. Strength is the ability to express an apology without expecting the recipient to accept it. Strength is proving that the essence of true power is reigning from within.

We all have those days that we forget to celebrate the progress and appreciate the setbacks. Each event is highly valuable to our character development. I have been in situations where my knees were wobbling out of control about to buckle under the pressure. It is in those moments that I reflect on the strength of innumerable women who have demonstrated mental toughness in a worse set of circumstances.

Strength can also be revealed in quiet assurance. A lion never has to roar for us to be aware that he has the capacity to do so. Allow yourself the free will to simply be. Remember, your presence is more powerful than fist pounding. In the words of Oscar Wilde, "We are all in the gutter, but some of us are looking at the stars."

Every day is an opportunity to become stronger in our beliefs, stronger in our tenacity, stronger in our hopes, stronger in our commitments, stronger in expressing ourselves to others, stronger in relinquishing fear of control, stronger in speaking our truth and stronger in caring for ourselves.

You are stronger than you feel, stronger than you think, stronger than you know and stronger than you believe. This test is here only to reveal a new you that has been waiting to breakthrough. Embrace today. Embrace the moment. Embrace the beauty. Embrace love. Embrace hope. Embrace the truth. Embrace everything that will thrust you forward.

C.P.I.L.L. Confidence Prescription for Progress

Crownfirmation: My spirit is massive and greater than the cocoon that has held me captive. I will spread my wings and dare to dream. The power of momentum is driven by my relentless actions towards building a stronger me.

Pause to Ponder: My greatest strength is: _____ and it often appears when:

I Celebrate:

Leadership Lesson Learned:

Lifestyle Elevation: Every Day I Will,

Day 43

Power

Implies possession of ability to wield force, authority, or influence. The right to do something.

Dear Queen,

Success alone is not enough because it is only one piece of the puzzle. Success without authentic power is futile. Authentic power is discovered in origination, never imitation. Power originates from having a voice and being able to effectuate change.

On a personal level, power is the ability to produce the results that we desire most. This ability begins by overcoming the mental barriers that impede success and raising personal expectations.

Susan Wilson Solovic says, "Power is also about granting yourself permission to be successful, to follow your passions and live out your dreams. You must turn off negative messages that dictate what you 'should' do, instead of what you want to do. Power comes from fearlessly taking risks and striving for excellence. Power hinges on economic freedom and broad personal networks. Finally, an essential element of power for women centers on our ability to work together to leverage our collective voices so that we can be the leaders of change and leave a lasting legacy for future generations."

Three ways to gain access to power:

1) **There is power in pausing**. A temporary stop in action. A brief suspension to indicate the limits. A short break. What does this look like? A cat nap, a walk at the park, meditation, a bubble bath or a night out with the girls, etc. Gracefully step away from the things that deplete your energy, challenge you, stress you, etc.

2) **There is power in pacing**. A consistent and continuous speed in moving. Pace comes from the Latin word Passus, meaning 'A step'. Pace is a noun, meaning 'the speed at which something happens'. Many women become overwhelmed because we try to do too much, too fast. All at once, then we burn and crash. It's about the quality of our contribution rather than the quantity of activities. Can you sustain the speed you are currently moving at over the long haul without damaging your mind, body, and soul?

3) **There is power in professing**. To affirm openly; declare or claim to admit publicly that you have a particular feeling or belief. What are you saying to yourself on a daily basis? My gratitude journaling class instructor said, "Just because your inner critic is in the car does not mean she gets to drive." Your inner critic will always have something to say, but you have the power to keep her at bay by putting her in place with words of positivity.

The truth is the firmest foundation on which you can stand. Authentic power is rooted in the courage to cleave to pure unadulterated truth. The ugliest parts of truth are often the shadows of your greatest strength. I love this quote by Amaka Imani Nkosazana. "You can push the truth off a cliff, but it will always fly. You can submerge the truth under water, but it will not drown. You can place the truth in the fire, but it will burn brighter. You can bury the truth beneath the ground, but it will rise high. Truth always prevails it needs no-one to defend."

Authentic power gives you the courage to tell the whole truth, embrace the whole truth and live for nothing but the whole truth. May you experience life to the full and walk with a vibrant elegance that radiates for all to see.

C.P.I.L.L. Confidence Prescription for Progress

Crownfirmation: I will exercise my power, execute my authority and eliminate my excuses.

Pause to Ponder: What does it mean to be powerful? How will you contribute to the global conversation and benefit society as a powerful instrument of transformation?

I Celebrate:

Leadership Lesson Learned:

Lifestyle Elevation: Every Day I Will,

Day 44

Challenge

A stimulating task or problem.

Dear Queen,

What I have come to understand is that greatness is often embedded in the grains of groaning, wisdom flows from a riverbed of weeping, and solitude rests upon the sunset of sorrow. Pain is an excruciating birth canal to purpose, prosperity, and prominence. It can be difficult to appreciate and articulate the gift it creates while sitting under its soul-crushing weight.

How do you remain steady in spirit when the storms of life blow relentlessly day and night? There seems to be no reprieve in sight. It is during the darkest moments of our lives that painstaking adversity inspires us to uncover our hidden magnificence. Dr. Cornel West painted the perfect picture. "Three pillars of deep spirituality are faith, hope, and love. Yet it is courage that enables all three. Spirituality gives us armor to cope with disaster. Faith enables us to face the future-including inescapable catastrophes-with humility and generosity. Yet there is no faith without the courage to be humble. Hope empowers us to stay on the tightrope despite the winds and storms of catastrophes. Yet there is no hope without the courage to fight despair. Love enables us to maintain a steadfast commitment to the well-being of someone or some cause greater than our own petty ego. Yet there is no love without the courage to surrender to something more priceless than yourself. Our unimagined victories in the face of catastrophic conditions are majestic evidence of a rich spiritual tradition. The question is never whether catastrophes will come but rather when they come, what choices will we make?"

How footloose and fancy-free would we be if our days were filled with sunshine and blue skies? What if we could wake everyday void of problems and not a care in the world? As long as we are alive in this world, we must become armed internally for battle against unending trials that test our resolve.

The definition of steady is to remain firmly fixed, balanced, stable, not shaking or moving. **When you are confronted with hardships that appear impossible to conquer, refuse to bow in defeat.**

Recently, I was inspired by words from an Adidas ad regarding the word impossible. It stated, "Impossible is a big word thrown around by small men who find it easier to live in the world they've been given than to explore the power they have to change it. Impossible is not a fact. It's an opinion. Impossible is not a declaration. It's a dare. Impossible is potential. Impossible is temporary. Impossible is nothing."

As you begin to move forward into greater realms of success and achievement, remain steady in your passion, in your purpose, and in your internal positioning. You were designed to triumph over troubles and soar over setbacks. A champion needs a challenge like a bird needs to sing, like a queen needs her bling, a champion needs a challenge like a car needs gas by the gallons, like a bee needs to sting and like a song needs a melody. **Don't hide from the inevitable; it's the very thing that makes you incredible.**

If you desire to live abundantly take a deep breath and heal the hurt, hold the lesson, harness the power of resilience and forgiveness. Re-imagine what's possible as you take a deeper look beneath the obstacles.

"The longer you have to wait for something, the more you will appreciate it when it finally arrives the harder you have to fight for something, the more priceless it will become once you achieve it. The more pain you have to endure on your journey, the sweeter the arrival at your destination. All good things are worth waiting for and worth fighting for."

–Susan Gale

C.P.I.L.L. Confidence Prescription for Progress

Crownfirmation: I am mentally, emotionally, spiritually and physically prepared to conquer every challenge that rises to deflate my energy as I press towards my destiny.

Pause to Ponder: Our challenges often come to reveal hidden weaknesses and awaken dormant strengths. Can you identify where you are vulnerable and the greatest strength you possess?

I Celebrate:

Leadership Lesson Learned:

Lifestyle Elevation: Every Day I Will,

Day 45

Reckoning

A settling of accounts

Dear Queen,

What internal resolve do you need to create a new way of living? There are gifts inside of you that have yet to be unwrapped. There are words of hope buried in your heart waiting to heal a broken soul. There are ideas that can change the course of this world.

I remember writing these words in my wellness journal in 2018, *'Change is critical. You need to make a lifestyle commitment to wellness, and it must become non-negotiable. You are playing Russian roulette with your health. The buck stops here with an unshakable decision.'* In the words of Cleopatra the Great, "I will not be triumphed over." I was not created to succumb to fear but designed to subdue fortresses." You must fight for what you believe in until the very end.

Do you believe that your brilliance will be instrumental in altering the destiny of innumerable lives? The fact that you are still alive should be provocation enough to rise as a torch of light shining brightly for those battling defeat to see. Joan of Arc was only thirteen years old when she responded to the voice of God to lead an army. She immediately discounted herself and began to focus on her inadequacies.

It's true; Joan was illiterate, she was a young girl, and she did not possess any military training. The one thing she did have was undeniable courage. She was born to lead, and all that was required was to say yes and declare it to be a day of reckoning for an army that was weak and in need of strong leadership. She led them to victory and was later burned to death for her convictions. In Joan's words, "Act, and God will act, work, and God will work."

You must sever the ties with anything that bind and blind you from the truth of who you are. Look yourself in the mirror and reiterate your call to be great.

I am as bold as a lion. Fear, timidity, and anxiety cannot abide inside of a heart filled with faith, tenacity and serenity. As I contemplate and sit, I must candidly admit that I am too legit to quit. I offer myself a verbal apology for living beneath infinite possibilities, beneath divine power, potential, prudence, and providence. To hide from the shadow of one's own majesty is a travesty of destiny. Let this be a day of reckoning a sweet hour of beckoning, a silent symphony to experience a once in a lifetime soul epiphany. That which one has been tailor-made to do, must not be refused. I have become my own muse. Do not seek to muzzle me because I was born to express the ornate tapestry of my creative mastery. Unapologetically shining brightly like a diamond in a dim and dark society...living boldly as God's unique and exquisite masterpiece. Let this be a day of reckoning for all to see.

C.P.I.L.L. Confidence Prescription for Progress

Crownfirmation: I have settled in my heart that I will fulfill my part in leaving an eternal mark of love in the earth.

Pause to Ponder: What cause have you embraced that is worth dying for, worth fighting for, worth living for, worth sacrificing for, worth suffering for, worth being ostracized for or worth being criticized for?

I Celebrate:

Leadership Lesson Learned:

Lifestyle Elevation: Every Day I Will,

Transformation

The act or process of changing completely.

Dear Queen,

Today is the day to raise your expectations. While you are waiting for change, your change is waiting for you. I received a message from a young lady that read, "I honestly have days where I feel like I lack the strength and stamina to keep moving forward."

As an empath, I am deeply aware of how emotions can lead you down a rabbit trail to nowhere. **If you find yourself in the valley of discouragement, look at the difficulty as an opportunity to embrace a new way to display your strength.**

We often want transformation to occur instantly. The first day you work out you want the scale to be ten pounds lighter. You gained fifty pounds over two years and for some reason you want it to disappear in a day. The process, which is defined as a series of actions, will require you to recommit continuously in order to transform completely.

The top cause for giving up on achieving the change we desire is that the results don't appear fast enough. Change is uncomfortable and to live in discomfort can become unbearable for the individual who does not have a strong enough reason to remain faithful to the goal. We also tend to put off transformation until we feel inspired to act. Your feelings will leave you disillusioned and stuck in the same place this time next year. **Transformation starts with a decision to do what is necessary for the entire duration until you witness the desired outcome.** The minute you get serious about creating a major lifestyle change, there is nothing that can dissuade you from moving forward.

When I decide to alter specific behavioral patterns, I do not seek out approval from any outside sources. I develop a plan of action and start executing immediately. It is best to act speedily on ideas because any distraction can deflate your motivation. As you identify what change needs to be made, don't aim for mediocre modifications pursue massive alterations that will provoke you to achieve exponential growth.

Here are three steps to transform powerfully into the leader you were born to be.

1) **Deconstruct.** Exposing internal assumptions and contradictions. Think about what you are thinking about and shift back into a positive state mind.

2) **Reconstruct.** To rebuild after damage. This is your chance to bounce back better than ever.

3) **Construct.** Mentally framing how you will live differently from this time forward.

C.P.I.L.L. Confidence Prescription for Progress

Crownfirmation: I am transforming through the renewing of my mind one positive thought and bold action step at a time.

Pause to Ponder: What is the most frustrating aspect of your personal transformation?

I Celebrate:

Leadership Lesson Learned:

Lifestyle Elevation: Every Day I Will,

Day 47

Destiny

A predetermined course of events often held to be an irresistible power or agency something foreordained and often suggests a great or noble course or end.

Dear Queen,

Own your lane and do it your way. Yes, you can glean from others who have gone before you, but never lose sight that no-one is you and that is your power. Embrace your unique brilliance and never be afraid of who you are destined to become. The most valuable lesson entrepreneurship has taught me is that there is no time like the present.

Are you ready to dance with destiny? The dance floor is all yours. Think about when you are invited to a night out on the town. There is usually a reason for the occasion, and that is what we call purpose. The blazing fire is burning in your soul to move.

The next thing we do in preparation is to find the perfect outfit. This represents your position. If you wear clothing that suggests that you are available those who see you might assume the same. Your position is what you stand for or believe in. If you believe you are a lady, your attire will reflect that position.

As you arrive at an event and mingle with others, the way you conduct yourself reflects your posture. Your appearance may say, "I'm a lady," but your actions may be contradictory, and it could leave others confused. Lastly, if you have positioned yourself appropriately, postured yourself accordingly and poised yourself correctly, you will be remembered powerfully.

The pattern of pursuing our destiny is no different. We prepare ourselves from childhood to the present moment to awaken the most powerful version of who we have yet to become. Truthfully speaking many will never walk in their full potential and reach their divine destiny because of the endless behind the scenes preparation that is required to attain greatness.

I often say that standing on stage is the easy part of professional speaking or a book signing. Speaking is the icing on the cake after extensive researching and writing. The grueling aspects of destiny are often hidden in the heat of the night. It's the moments when you are staring at your fears as your eyes are burning from dream building. Disciplining your body to eat only fruits, vegetables, nuts, and oatmeal while training five to six days a week to ensure your blood pressure remains low. There is a secret cost to pay and it is the only thing that counts if you plan to cross the finish line.

In order to fulfill your divine destiny, it will require you being deliberate in how you manage your time. You will need to pay close attention to the details of every interaction and life experience. Be mindful of who you are discussing your future plans with. Expect delays and be ready to implement a contingency plan immediately.

As you move towards your divine destiny be aware of friction which is defined as resistance to motion or conflict of one object relative to another. In the end, it's all good because friction produces conviction and conviction fuels massive momentum.

Keep dreaming, keep dancing and keep doing what you do. There are no riches above a sound body and no joy above the happiness of the heart.

C.P.I.L.L. Confidence Prescription for Progress

Crownfirmation: I am not afraid of who I am. I embrace every aspect of my being. The world is my runway and my dreams are escorting me to destiny.

Pause to Ponder: Express clearly what you perceive your divine destiny to be. Examine every single experience and connect the dots. There is a central theme that will reveal exactly why you are here and who needs what you have to give.

I Celebrate:

Leadership Lesson Learned:

Lifestyle Elevation: Every Day I Will,

Day 48

Believe

To consider to be true or honest, to accept the word or evidence of, to have a firm or wholehearted religious conviction or persuasion, to have faith or confidence in the existence or worth of.

Dear Queen,

The triplets of hope are faith, belief, and imagination. Faith is the lead character in the dramatic chronicles of my life. She is a dedicated supporter cheering me on to unfathomable heights. She is a quiet whisper piercing through the shadows of the night. She is the scribe behind the pen that allows me to write with such delight. She is my constant companion, who reminds me to courageously dance to the rhythm of my own beat. When I sit in silence to ponder alone, it is the sound of her voice bellowing in my ear, "You are a champion." She is the beauty I see when the world is a beast. She is the beginning, middle, and end. **Faith is ever present and ever ready to revive, restructure and reward me with an intangible prize for remaining in the fight.** Her prominent role is a major force in cultivating all that I have become and all I that I hope to be.

Oprah Winfrey said, "It's not only noble to have strong beliefs, it's necessary. It's even far more powerful to back up those beliefs with action. What are you willing to stand up for? Do your beliefs matter to you enough that you'd publicly defend them? How much would you put on the line to do so?"

Belief stands on the shoulders of faith when the light of expectation begins to fade. It is in the center of belief that we hold fast to the profession of our faith until it silences the storm. The pillow top of belief brings rest to the tired soul ready to let it all go.

Then there is the miraculous manifestation which is a byproduct of a vivid imagination. The definition of imagination is the action of forming new ideas, images or concepts of external objects not present to the senses and the power to be creative or resourceful. Imagination is the ability to picture yourself differently and become whatever you see.

Unstoppable belief must run deep in your bones, beneath an acute internal awareness and alignment that will lead to the attainment of the sweetest desires. Believe as long as you must believe. I chose not to date for thirteen years, and one day my future husband was sitting in a business seminar across the room from me. The rest is history.

I challenge you to believe when life is great. Believe when the bills must be paid. Believe when it seems hard to find your way. Believe until you see a brighter day. Believe after a broken heart and believe when you discover the missing part. Believe when you feel alone and believe when there is standing room only. Believe when there are no deadlines to meet and believe when there is not enough help to achieve your goals with speed.

Before you close your eyes tonight, clasp tightly to faith in your dreams, believe in yourself and soar on the wings of your wildest imaginations.

C.P.I.L.L. Confidence Prescription for Progress

Crownfirmation: I believe I possess the internal key to unlock the doors to extraordinary achievements beyond what I have ever imagined or dreamed.

Pause to Ponder: Write out your top ten beliefs that are the cornerstone to how you lead.

I Celebrate:

Leadership Lesson Learned:

Lifestyle Elevation: Every Day I Will,

Day 49

Lead

To direct the operations, activity, or performance of, to be first to direct in a course or show the way to be followed. Intimate knowledge of the way and of all its difficulties and dangers. Implies showing the way and often keeping those that follow under control and in order. An ability to keep to a course and stresses the capacity of maneuvering correctly. Suggests guidance over a dangerous or complicated course.

Dear Queen,

Stop masquerading. You are the only one who can lead in the starring role of your life. Who could honestly be internally satisfied with sitting on the sidelines watching limitless opportunities pass by?

Every leading lady must practice her lines until they are completely memorized if she is going to radiantly shine during show time. Are you reading the role of victim or victor? Here is the bottom line. **You can either stay stuck in your sorrow or showcase your power**. I place my bet on your brilliance and resilience.

Alex Gray stated, "The top three effective leadership traits of female leaders are: Leading by example, open and honest communication and humble enough to admit mistakes."

It typically takes years to master a craft and convert your passion into a profit bearing business. After building and developing a vision from the ground up consistently day after day, it is understandable if you find yourself disconnected from your original goal. If you find yourself in an emotional lull and disengaged, it may be time to create a quiet space for reflection and begin asking questions to reignite your internal fire.

Before you embark on a new voyage towards personal development and goal attainment, it is vital that you recognize the race is not given to the swift, nor the strong but to the one who is able to mentally endure seasons of hardships until success is sure.

At the center of your being, and apart from titles, who are you? As you pursue your purpose, there will be insurmountable obstacles that cause you to doubt your skills and ability to finish the course. The challenges of life may create chasms in your confidence level that cripple your drive. You will have to muster every ounce of strength to fight for your divine destiny. Adversity will leave you grasping for the slightest inch of hope. The key to persevering is determination and refusing to give up no matter what comes or who goes.

Do you know where you are going?

The power of vision will provide a second wind to propel you further than you could ever envision possible. In the midst of complexities, it is easy to sink into despair, but it is at the crossroads of calamity that you either remain stuck in a rut or allow the tumultuous storm to catapult you into unimaginable altitudes of achievement.

We know that an automobile operates by gasoline and when it runs out, we value having a full tank of fuel even more. Over the course of time, you will travel many miles and find yourself running on fumes from the distance covered. When your enthusiasm begins to subside, ask yourself why is it important to lead others?

"The world is changed by your example, not your opinion."

–Paul Coelho

At this juncture, it is critical to reassess why you wake up every morning, how many lives you've impacted through your unwavering courage to lead, the rewards of being authentically you, and the benefits you will reap in daring to follow your dreams until they come true.

If it were easy anyone would do it, but you are a rare and peculiar piece of fabric, a cut above all that is commonly average. **Dig deep within and find that flame of passion for making a difference.**

In the words of the late Steve Jobs, "Here's to the crazy ones, the misfits, the rebels, the troublemakers, the round pegs in the square holes, the ones who see things differently—they're not fond of rules. You can quote them, disagree with them, glorify or vilify them, but the only thing you can't do is ignore them because they change things. They push the human race forward, and while some may see them as the crazy ones, we see genius, because the ones who are crazy enough to think that they can change the world, are the ones who do."

C.P.I.L.L. Confidence Prescription for Progress

Crownfirmation: I will lead others in the spirit of excellence, honor and unquestionable integrity. I am the difference maker and thought shaper of impressionable minds that expect a role model who is uncompromised in character or wise advice.

Pause to Ponder: Have you assessed your own leadership qualities that make you an asset to any team? How will you convert your ideas into influence and impact history?

I Celebrate:

Leadership Lesson Learned:

Lifestyle Elevation: Every Day I Will,

Day 50

Rest

Freedom from activity or labor. A state of motionlessness or inactivity, free of anxieties. To spend time relaxing, sleeping, or doing nothing after you have been active or doing work.

Dear Queen,

Your mental and emotional health depends on you take time to pause and catch your breath. As a woman who wears too many crowns with numerous tasks waiting to be done, one is bound to fall off.

How can you maintain and sustain a lifestyle of balance in the whirlwind of busyness? I feel it is vital to first start with the definition of maintain, which means: to preserve from failure, or decline, to sustain against opposition, to carry on, to keep in a current state of order, to prevent from falling apart or breaking down and to take care of.

When you get tired, learn to rest, not quit. Hit the reset button and celebrate every single door opened. It is a sacred privilege to honor your body for the daily strength it brings.

"There is a pleasure in the pathless woods, there is a rapture on the lonely shore, there is society, where none intrudes, by the deep sea, and music in its roar: I love not man the less, but nature more."

–Lord Byron

Maintaining balance is an everyday challenge that requires a commitment to make frequent mental adjustments and to choose wisely which activities I will selectively entertain. In my bourgeoning evolution as an entrepreneur, I loved the thrill of pursuing a new idea and opportunity often at the expense of my own wellness.

As a maturing leader, I have developed clearer boundaries and established value-driven priorities to reinforce the importance of maintaining balance in mind, body, and soul. What does that look like? Exercising frequently. Eating healthier. Pampering myself with massages or pedicures. Walks in the park with my dog. Quality time with my loving husband. Keeping in touch with covenant connections. Investing in self-development. Quiet time to reflect in prayer and commune with God. Adequate rest and relaxation. Fun and laughter. Essentially, what it boils down to is a conscientious decision to work hard and play harder.

Complete the Ready for Rest Self-Check to ascertain your current emotional state:

I am feeling sleep deprived and only get about four to six hours of rest each night? Circle Yes or No

Usually, I have an upbeat personality, but lately, I am feeling snappy and unhappy. Circle Yes or No

The work I do used to bring me joy, and now it feels more like a dreaded chore. Circle Yes or No

Due to the demands of my job or business, I have no free time to connect with friends, participate in physical activity or savor the simple pleasures of life. Circle Yes or No

It can be difficult to say no to requests for my time, and I now find myself overbooked and overwhelmed. Circle Yes or No

If you circled yes more than no, take a moment to identify new patterns of behavior that will provide valuable space to rejuvenate and regenerate. In the words of Etty Hillesum, "Sometimes the most important thing in a whole day is the rest we take between two deep breaths."

C.P.I.L.L. Confidence Prescription for Progress

Crownfirmation: I was not created to break down, I was born to break through. I disconnect from any individual who desires to exploit my gifts for their own personal gain and deliberately gravitate towards soul enrichers who seek to empower my genius which fuels boundless potential and possibilities. I commit to strengthening these social leadership traits until they are deeply ingrained inside of me.

Pause to Ponder: Get an index card and write out the top ten healthy habits you desire to exhibit every day and at the end of the day give yourself a grade ranging from a-f. The goal is to be a straight a student in your life.

Example of how this looks:

EVERY DAY I: pray and meditate

EVERY DAY I: honor my spouse

EVERY DAY I: eat wholesome foods

I Celebrate:

Leadership Lesson Learned:

Lifestyle Elevation: Every Day I Will,

Day 51

Steadfast

Firm in belief, determination, or adherence.

Dear Queen,

Steadfastness gives you the strength to conquer new feats. How do you remain steady in spirit when the storms of life blow relentlessly day and night? There seems to be no reprieve in sight. It is during the darkest moments of our lives that painstaking adversity inspires us to uncover our hidden magnificence.

There is freedom waiting for you on the breezes of the sky, and you ask, "What if I fall?" In the words of Erin Hanson, "Oh but darling, what if you fly?" **There is victory in the valley, and you can be triumphant in trouble**. Focus on the metamorphosis occurring on the inside, not the temporary discomfort transpiring on the outside.

Stand still and embrace your victory.

Trust in the midst of uncertain times.

Expect abundant blessings to greet you daily.

Always seek to have a positive outlook on life.

Declare goodness and favor as your divine inheritance.

Yield to the process of becoming a catalyst of greatness.

Aim to deepen your presence as you hone key skills needed on the path to greatness. A true leader has the capacity to ignite more than their own vision. It takes discipline of thought to continually focus on conquering the goal set before you. You need to see everything else as a distraction or temporary obstacle capable of being removed by the power of God's eternal word. If God be for you, who or what dare stand against you?

Can you see increase in the face of lack? Can you embrace victory in the face of defeat? Can you expect healing when fighting an illness? Can you receive joy in your soul when the spirit of depression is chasing you like a bandit?

Until you can, obstacles will constantly impede your growth in the process of dream development.

It is important that you find out where you are in your own journey towards greatness. Always remember, the possibilities are infinite.

C.P.I.L.L. Confidence Prescription for Progress

Crownfirmation: As my dream unfolds, I am willing to remain unyielding in focus no matter how bone-shaking the road to greatness becomes. I am devoted to the task and determined to remain steadfast in confident belief.

Pause to Ponder: If you were to place your fulfilled dreams on a billboard what would every car passing by see? What are your greatest insights gained during the course of this year? What obstacles did you encounter inside yourself? In which areas of your life do you wish you spent less or more time? What will you do differently this month?

I Celebrate:

Leadership Lesson Learned:

Lifestyle Elevation: Every Day I Will,

Day 52

Become

To undergo change or development, to be suitable, or to look attractive on (someone).

Dear Queen,

Countless souls have yet to embrace their essence because they fear the empty minded critics. I've been a prisoner inside my own thoughts, and I understand the invisible fight. What I have resolved to do is not give negativity a platform in my life. Speak your truth and shatter the chains of limitation.

Joel Osteen wrote in his book I Declare, "We need to become dispensers of good." As humans, the natural response when the storms of life come is to clam up and go inside. I've been saying to myself lately, it's not in your knowing, it's in your doing. That's where the power lies.

There is always an aspect of ourselves that can be enhanced, and it is essential that we surround ourselves with those who are fanatics of focus. To become requires an outlandish commitment to change.

In the days of my youth, I was known for having a negative attitude and a short fuse. It became more important that I loved the woman in the mirror more than the outside world could affirm me. I began to study female leaders who were graceful and watch video interviews to see how they conducted themselves. How did they dress? How did they sit? How did they respond to applause? How did they handle critics? Excellence leaves a pattern that is easy to model.

The beauty of becoming is when you embody everything you've aspired to be. The definition of embody means to be an expression of, represent, give tangible or visible form to, exemplify, personify or fill the role completely.

The benefit of becoming is the gift of influence. As a global voice of honorable distinction, the message is clear, the messenger is credible, and the motive is compassion driven. This is why we invest in ourselves and live a life that is worthy of adulation.

C.P.I.L.L. Confidence Prescription for Progress

Crownfirmation: As I become, the world stands up and takes notice of the hidden work I've done.

Pause to Ponder: In what ways will you deliberately be the change, be the light, be the healer, be the good, be the door, be the miracle, be the hope, be the friend, be the investor, be the encourager, be the guide, be the truth, be the lifeline, be the leader and beat average?

I Celebrate:

Leadership Lesson Learned:

Lifestyle Elevation: Every Day I Will,

Awaken

To wake up or to rouse from sleep.

Dear Queen,

The moment you confront the shadows of your past, you can boldly embrace a new dawn that is always within grasp. Are you ready to grace major platforms reserved only for you? Next level is here. With the world as your runway, walk powerfully and purposefully into new stratospheres of influence. Beat average in all you do and allow magnificence to be your stamp of approval.

"When you are evolving into a higher-self, the road may seem lonely, but you're simply shedding the energies that no longer match the frequency of your destiny."

–Unknown

To awaken is to discover that what was holding you back and to perceive a new trail to blaze. The world may sleep on your greatness, but you cannot allow yourself to live in a comatose state. The scope of contributions that we make to our society will be a direct reflection of our personal awakening. In the words of W. Clement Stone, "Definiteness of purpose is the starting point of all achievement." I believe it is far more important to understand who you are before you can fully embrace where you are going.

One of the ways I shake myself from slumber is to stand in front of the mirror, look deeply into my eyes, and speak from the heart until I cry. To provoke myself to complete a project I may say, "You have done this three times before. Finish what you started. Now is not the time to give up. Finish what you started. There is more inside of you. Finish what you started. The celebratory party is waiting for you. Finish what you started. Lives are at stake. Finish what you started. Elevate to great and finish what you started."

I will not rely on someone else to light my fire when I carry my own set of matches. **Sleepwalkers never make record-breaking history, only those who aware, awake and ready to shake the earth with their superpowers.** Awaken the best parts of you, awaken the strength concealed inside, awaken the dreams that have taken a nap, awaken the tenacity to fight for your prosperity and awaken every ounce of potential that has hit the snooze button. The time is now; there is much to gain and nothing to lose.

C.P.I.L.L. Confidence Prescription for Progress

Crownfirmation: I will awaken my spirit to seize the goals in front of me. I am wide awake to my potential to be great.

Pause to Ponder: If I could only spend my time doing three things what would they be?" For wellness sake, eliminate the non-essentials.

I Celebrate:

Leadership Lesson Learned:

Lifestyle Elevation: Every Day I Will,

Tenacity

Mental or moral strength to resist opposition, danger, or hardship. Courage implies firmness of mind and will in the face of danger or extreme difficulty. An ingrained capacity for meeting strain or difficulty with fortitude and resilience.

Dear Queen,

You can withstand the scorching hot desert sands because the heat is exactly what you need to fuel your feet for the next galactic feat. Stay prepared to walk through doors you've sought to open and sit at tables you never asked to eat.

As a first-generation full-time entrepreneur tenacity is a must or I would crumble along the wayside of defeat. Every day I elevate my mental state from good to great. **There is no such thing as an overnight success, despite the seducing media advertisements.** I currently have seventeen vision boards posted on my office wall and five vision books to stay motivated. I know firsthand that having a strong mind is critical to rising above insurmountable obstacles.

You will need tenacity to break through every barrier of adversity. Tenacity is defined as to keep a firm hold of something; clinging or adhering closely, not readily relinquishing a course of action and remaining determined.

When I was younger, I battled low self-esteem and depression, which led to substance abuse to numb the pain. It was only a temporary solution to a more pervasive issue. One day I decided I wanted to be a positive role model for other women. I began to work on my attitude day by day. **Every negative experience is an invitation for elevation, not condemnation or incapacitation.**

Having a tenacious spirit allowed me to go to Bangkok, Thailand shortly after I lost everything in my second business launch. It allowed me to endure five years of suffering through anemia and seven uterine fibroid tumors. Tenacity allowed me to overcome high blood pressure and not have to take medication prescribed by medical doctors. Tenacity allowed me to overcome financial hardships and continue to create in the midst of uncertainty. It allowed me to create my newest company after being terminated in 2015. It allowed me to re-invent myself after losing my speaking agent of four years and it keeps me strong during every changing season of life.

You possess the heart of a champion, and the power to outlive it all. Warriors don't die, they intensify, fortify, multiply until they occupy. In the fight of your life never run and hide. Leadership development is inexhaustible. It is dangerous to think you've got it all together no matter how long you've stood at the helm.

I was reading Mentoring Leaders by Carson Pue, and he stated, "Many leaders are too busy for feedback. They often start believing their own press and rarely have time to reflect." This can result in losing themselves. I'm in the business of winning, and I have one goal: elevate to great every single day.

Understand this; broken pieces make the most magnificent creations. Your pain will serve a greater purpose. You may not understand now but you will appreciate the future tapestry of beauty as it unfolds. Snatch your tenacity back and live again.

Live BIGGER than your fears.

Live LOUDER than your pain.

Live BOLDER than your doubts.

Live STRONGER than your struggle.

Live GREATER than your groaning.

Live HAPPIER than your sorrow.

Live LONGER than your setbacks.

Live WILDER than your limitations.

Finally, always remember nothing massive ever occurred by being passive. The world is a jungle either you fight and elevate or hide and dissipate.

C.P.I.L.L. Confidence Prescription for Progress

Crownfirmation: My mouth is a new sharp threshing instrument powerful enough to turn mountains into pixie dust. I possess the power and strength of 49 million. I will redeem the dream with relentless perseverance, determination, and unstoppable tenacity.

Pause to Ponder:

Why am I here?

Where am I now?

Who am I becoming?

I Celebrate:

Leadership Lesson Learned:

Lifestyle Elevation: Every Day I Will,

Day 55

Speak

To say something in order to convey information, thoughts, opinions, or feelings.

Dear Queen,

Do you ever wonder how it would feel to speak your personal truth to the masses? If you had the opportunity to stand before a large audience, what powerful life lesson would you share? Have you secretly desired to use your voice to make a difference in the minds of others? What is holding you back from unleashing your gift of greatness to the world?

In order to move forward purposefully towards the future, you must grasp the treasures of wisdom from your past. It has been stated that history repeats itself, and if you have painstaking memories of failure, it can often hinder your ability to experience uncommon success. You will never be able to share your story from the penthouse of power, if your mind is trapped in the little house of horrors.

I will never forget the many years I allowed my voice to dwell in a cave of silence because I was too afraid to set it free. The moment I courageously opened my mouth despite trepidation changed my life forever. It is selfish to withhold our gifts from others, and it is noble to generously share.

We each hold a unique set of keys designed to unlock our divine destiny, and there are unlimited doors of opportunities waiting for us to fearlessly march through.

Here are three action steps to discover your authentic speaking voice:

1) **Practice the art of journaling**. As you reflect on your journal entries what message continues to reappear?

2) **Observe conversations**. As you communicate with others what topic do you find yourself speaking about the most? What subject matter do you gravitate towards frequently? What are people affirming about you and your passionate views?

3) **Speak constantly**. You must be willing to start somewhere. In order to have a commanding presence and speak with authority, you must hone your craft.

The perfect time to act will always be in the moment, take center stage and own it.

"Speak your mind, even if your voice shakes."

–Maggie Kuhn

When you become a voice and not an echo, you won't look for excitement; you will be excitement. You are not looking to be motivated; you are motivation. You are not looking to be empowered; you are empowerment. You are not looking to be inspired; you are inspiration. You are not looking to be accepted; you are acceptance. You are not looking to be fulfilled; you are fulfillment. Everything you need is awakened by the words you speak.

Until you find your voice, your thoughts are co-dependent on someone else speaking for you. The problem with that is, you might not agree with what's being said. Your silence saves no-one and shifts nothing. Your voice is yours to own. Yours to love. Yours to appreciate. Yours to reveal. Yours to understand. Yours to impact. Yours to feel. Yours to live. Yours to re-write. Yours to honor. Yours to protect. Yours to hold and never let go of.

C.P.I.L.L. Confidence Prescription for Progress

Crownfirmation: Loving myself is one of life's richest rewards and using my voice is the catalyst to an irrefutable revolution.

Pause to Ponder: If stepped outside of yourself and whispered into your own ear, what words of affirmation would you be encouraged to hear?

I Celebrate:

Leadership Lesson Learned:

Lifestyle Elevation: Every Day I Will,

Day 56

Progress

A royal journey, an onward movement forward, to cultivate to a higher, better, or more advanced life.

Dear Queen,

How do you continue to tread forward when you're surrounded by a forest of uncertainty? The moment you make progress in your daily mission, there is nothing that can thwart your intentions. After I received the pink slip, I chose to focus on what was before me, not what was behind me. It is easy to replay the memories of yesterday, but they will only delay your opportunity to be great.

Progressive-minded individuals have mastered the discipline of consistency. It's doing the same thing repeatedly until you accomplish your goal. I used to wonder how my husband could eat the same meal (chicken and white rice) day after day. His focus was on fueling his body for optimal performance in the gym and eating reasonable portions that were guaranteed to burn off during his weightlifting session. He was not concerned with taste, just the necessary nutrients to stay in the best shape.

This is how progress is made, by taking the unpopular route of discomfort. It's doing what average minds refuse to do and reaping uncommon rewards on the back end in exchange for an upfront investment. We've read that it takes twenty-one days to change a habit, but there are alternate studies that show it is typically around sixty-six days for a new habit to become ingrained. Could your lack of progress reflect your lack of commitment?

Albert Einstein said, "Great spirits have always encountered violent opposition from mediocre minds." The moment you take a stand for something more powerful than yourself be prepared for war. Common weapons used by rulers of darkness and spiritual wickedness in high places are soul-crushing words. Progress is often paralyzed by destructive words of disbelief in our abilities.

You need an unwavering conviction that refuses to flinch in the face of conflict. If someone does not believe in your dream, your mission, or your purpose, you must shake the dust off your feet and keep moving forward. In the face of danger, keep moving forward. In the face of anger, keep moving forward. Under the canopy of confusion, keep moving forward. In the face of pain, keep moving forward until your progress is indisputable. As a voice of change, remember you didn't sign up to walk on easy street. Progress is the power to prevail even in the wilderness.

C.P.I.L.L. Confidence Prescription for Progress

Crownfirmation: I am progressive. I am prosperous. I am prolific.

Pause to Ponder: What three changes would you make in your life if you knew you had the support to make the changes correctly? Have you lost the fervency of passion, as a result of neglecting to do what makes you internally happy? If so, purposefully evaluate the value of each day, examine your self-sabotaging ways and execute definitive goals without a single delay.

I Celebrate:

Leadership Lesson Learned:

Lifestyle Elevation: Every Day I Will,

Day 57

Brilliant

Very bright, distinguished by unusual mental keenness or glowing with a high degree of light. Brilliant implies intense often sparkling brightness.

Dear Queen,

Faux societal labels serve one goal: to disable your growth and decrease the awareness of your true self-worth. What I have come to ascertain for myself is that one of the most significant accomplishments is to live single-minded in a world that promotes dual-mindedness. I am grateful for the ability to understand that imagination is the gateway to elevation.

As a leader, I must constantly reiterate to my insecurities that I am brilliant by design. When I was younger, my esteem was affected by standardized tests that I failed. I allowed them to make me believe I was less than great. The voice of brilliance began to advocate for me even when I did not believe. Brendon Burchard stated that "amplifying what is great within you will accelerate your life faster than trying to fix what you think limits you."

I am always seeking to find a gateway to greatness where there may only appear to be walls in front of me. In tech, a gateway is defined as a network node that connects two networks using different protocols together. In contrast, a bridge is used to join two similar types of networks. A gateway uses two dissimilar networks. This is how I interpret it for real life:

Adversity + opportunity = the perfect partners to produce uncommon feats.

Adversity holds the key to limitless possibilities, but you must open your eyes and seize. A gateway also means a tall and wide entrance which you must go through to get to another place. It would be refreshingly pleasant if we could only swim through cool waters to destiny, but the reality is fire awaits. Your brilliance is unquestionable, co-sign your own purpose, power, and potential.

When we use our cognitive faculties to envision what's next, we make full proof of our brilliance. Find out who you have yet to become. Upon discovery, fiercely love her, fight for her and let majesty arise in her.

The brilliant leader has mastered mind over matter,

equipped with the intellectual capacity

to produce results in the most chaotic conditions.

The brilliant leader is designed to last,

structured with a hard drive to succeed

where many fail to keep pace

because they expressively progress to fast.

The brilliant leader is creative in crisis,

a pioneer unafraid to delve into unchartered territories

where most hidden treasures are deeply stored.

The brilliant leader thrives off ingenuity,

spontaneity and is marked by a strong sense of individuality

to avoid becoming a carbon copy of someone else's reality.

C.P.I.L.L. Confidence Prescription for Progress

Crownfirmation: My aspirations are too grand to entertain limitations. I am an anomaly. Sophisticated complexity, reigning in paradigm shattering liberty. Those who study me will never reach the peak. I am in constant pursuit of mastery, ever ascending with each thought I think. I am an anomaly, destined to shift history. Fire breathing intensity, strong enough to consume defeat. I am an anomaly. Don't try to figure me out; it may leave you lost at sea.

Pause to Ponder: Where do you believe your brilliance shines the brightest?

I Celebrate:

Leadership Lesson Learned:

Lifestyle Elevation: Every Day I Will,

Day 58

Prepare

To make ready beforehand for some purpose, use, or activity to put in a proper state of mind to work out the details of: plan in advance to make yourself ready for something that you will be doing, something that you expect to happen.

Dear Queen,

Are you prepared to possess what you've been confessing? Get ready to take your next best step in a different direction as you switch your gaze towards extraordinary. Instead of merely choosing to exist, I urge you to experience life. I urge you to live. The next level leader is not only ready for change, but is ready to change. Get this: **change demands change**.

Preparation precedes opportunity. It always has and always will be the pattern for those who desire to achieve great things. My mother prepared me for adulthood by placing me in pageants at a young age. Through the pageant system, I learned how to walk with poise. I learned how to speak with grace. I learned how to choose the best clothes. I learned how to interact with others. I learned how to graciously accept loss. I learned how to cultivate a positive attitude, and I learned how to rise above my weaknesses.

Each one of those positive qualities gained were a part of my preparation to be the leader I am today. I didn't see the significance during that time and space. We often discount the value of preparation because of the innumerable hours of development. Preparation is the seed and success is the harvest. What do you desire to manifest? Average or amazing?

Decide to do what is necessary even if it seems uncomfortable. It will be a lonely walk in the beginning, but in the end, every sacrifice will be well worth the rewards. Your life deserves all of you and nothing less. Your future is dependent on the intentional moves you make consistently. The next level is contingent upon you severing ties with the old lies you've come to own as the truth.

I have kept a record of my accomplishments, certifications, speaking engagements, and public appearances because each one prepares me for greater opportunities to achieve. I see them as steppingstones to greatness.

To live prepared is to remain ready to lay claim on everything that is labeled with your name on it. If you prepare your healthy meals in advance, you will be ready to conquer your cravings. If you prepare your mind in the morning, you will be ready to overcome negativity in any environment. If you prepare your budget, you will be ready for a vacation in the summer. If you prepare your heart, you will be ready to fall in love. If you prepare yourself, you will be ready to grip success.

C.P.I.L.L. Confidence Prescription for Progress

Crownfirmation: I am prepared for the best life has to offer and I am ready to work with excellence until it shows up in my lap.

Pause to Ponder: What is the number one goal you desire to achieve in the next thirty days? What preparation is needed to guarantee success is achieved?

I Celebrate:

Leadership Lesson Learned:

Lifestyle Elevation: Every Day I Will,

Self-Care

To care for oneself.

Dear Queen,

As productive leaders, we are masters of execution but often novices in self-care. The beautiful gift of a brand-new day is a precious opportunity to change. It has been said that strong rocks need a soft place to rest. **Will you give yourself the gift of gentleness that you freely give to others?** The vehicle is just as important as the destination. It's time to thrive not just work your body into the ground to survive.

During my single years, I began to learn the art of self-care. I distinctly remember purchasing a huge teddy bear on Valentine's day. Loving others starts with spoiling yourself first. I am grateful for those days because this life skill is vital to be the best I can be for my husband.

I remember one of the first group coaching programs I was a part of where I learned the value of self-care. During that time, my life was topsy-turvy to say the least. The facilitator would start our session asking us to complete the sentence, "What I need right now is..." For years I was taught to focus on serving others. I am quite sure you've heard this before; be selfless, that's what leaders do. It was hard for me to identify what I needed. I will never forget the priceless moment of giving myself permission to be there for me. Now it's as natural as breathing.

All that happens externally is directed towards one thing, and that is dethroning the internal seat of power, your heart. Guard it with all diligence for out of it flows the issues of life.

One of the most common issues influential leaders must combat is mental fatigue. I know you think our armor is impenetrable and we never fall after leaping tall buildings in a single bound. If you are in any position of authority, it is vital to remain aware of key signs that indicate it is time to relax and unwind.

The demands, pressure and constant race to reach new finish lines can weary even the most resilient minds. The call to leadership is a commitment to sacrificial living. We find great fulfillment in giving, sharing and empowering others to attain their heartfelt desires.

Did you know that tending to your inner needs is just as important as caring for others? The problem occurs when we fail to realize that we are pouring stale air out of empty cups into barren souls who will always hunger for more, more and more.

The beauty of self-care allows us to re-align our life by design not default. It is rooted in a decision to be intentional about personal wellness as we define what matters most to us on an individual level. How long has it been since you've carved out a sacred space to love yourself lavishly?

Let's start with identifying what 'me' time looks like:

- Me time an uninterrupted block of time reserved for personal relaxation and enjoyment.

- Me time is the time you take to take care of yourself.

- It is the time you take to escape from the pressures of everyday life to make yourself whole where you are broken.

- Ideally, me time is something you do every day, maybe even several times a day.

- Me time enables you to love yourself first.

- Me time recharges your battery and allows you to quietly focus your attention on what is important. We become calm and centered and better able to deal with the painstaking bumps along the road of life.

- Me time is an investment in yourself, for yourself.

- Me time reminds you that you are not your work.

Finally, in the words of Alison Darrow, "If all you do is work, work, work, work, and no play... life ceases to be rewarding and becomes a dreary struggle."

C.P.I.L.L. Confidence Prescription for Progress

Crownfirmation: I will eliminate the non-essentials in order to experience electrified euphoria every day.

Pause to Ponder:

1) Write down three time robbers you are presently experiencing and eliminate immediately.

2) List three activities you would like to substitute for added internal satisfaction.

I Celebrate:

Leadership Lesson Learned:

Lifestyle Elevation: Every Day I Will,

Past

Time gone by, something that happened or was done in the past an earlier time, the time before the present.

Dear Queen,

Over twenty years ago, my self-esteem was dirt low after making one bad decision after the next. I dated the wrong men who did not value me because I did not value myself. To mask the pain, I would attempt to hide it in a bottle of alcohol or smoke it away. When I woke up guess who was looking back in my face? Me. We can't outrun ourselves. I decided to love myself and love her fiercely.

The greatest act of love is forgiveness. One of the most crippling emotions I have ever felt was shame. At the age of seventeen, I lost my virginity and became pregnant—all in one night. Mentally, I was in no condition to have a child. I made a selfish choice to have an abortion, and at the clinic, there were protestors outside. One of them handed me a little plastic doll to demonstrate I would be taking a human life. I kept that doll hidden in my lingerie drawer for two decades until going on a seventy-three day fast from comfort foods to atone for a decision I could never change.

Instantly, the emotional chains broke. I finally threw the doll away and forgave myself completely. Shame maintains control over that which we fear to speak about. I decided to live free from fear, judgment, condemnation and the opinion of others. Imperfection is my superpower. Truth is the most solid ground you can stand upon.

How long will you cry over spilled milk? **When you emotionally detach yourself from the situation, the solution becomes easily recognizable.** You can choose to wipe it up, throw it out, let it go and move on.

What if we could reframe the word failure and say that it is merely a resistance test. A pop quiz to see how fast you can bounce back from adversity. Disappointments are designed to unearth hidden treasures buried within our souls and we must courageously dig deep to bring them forth. Research shows individuals who have high self-esteem handle hardships with greater ease than those with low self-worth.

Are you afraid of being happy? This is what keeps you bound to the past. It's hard to move forward if you are always looking backward. The past can affect your psychological disposition negatively or positively. How are you showing up in the story of your life?

Addictions come in various forms, and we can be addicted to the past which is merely the story we tell ourselves regarding events we've experienced. Repeating old narratives will only create unwanted realities. What you speak, you breathe life into. Resuscitating the past is like digging up old rotten trash and placing it in the refrigerator.

Three main roles we play in the story of our life:

1) **Victim**. A person who has been harmed or injured as a result of an event or action. How long are you going to lick your wounds? (You turn inward—depression despair defeat etc.)

2) **Villain**. A cruelly malicious person, who does mean and evil things on purpose. A character who opposes the hero-which would be self-sabotage. (You turn outward-rage-anger attacking or punishing others for something they never caused.)

3) **Victor**. Latin for vincere-to conquer, to win, a person who defeats an enemy or opponent in a battle. One that requires physical strength or skills, one who triumphs over a difficult situation. (You turn upward—recognizing God is a very present help in the time of trouble.)

Every TV show has commercial breaks. We can use the power of a pause to interrupt and correct faulty thought patterns that automatically play in our minds.

Recently an old story that I had to bury was when I was stressed, I needed a treat. Continuously giving into to cravings ultimately led to high blood pressure.

I began to tell myself the danger of eating unhealthy foods is greater than the desire to experience temporary pleasure. I created vision board number sixteen after my blood pressure was at its highest and centered it around the theme, Boss of My Body. The focus was to incite an even more dedicated lifestyle of wellness.

Until you make peace with the pain of your past, what you see on a daily will be skewed. Without keen sight (internal vision) you lose strength to stand against the storms of life.

Ultimately, you will find yourself stuck in a rut, repeating the same sad song like a broken record. How do we shift from stuck to unstoppable and defy the impossible? By focusing on the beauty of your dreams.

How do you move beyond the past?

Face your fear, failure, and frustration. You must confront it and look it dead in the eyes. Learn to laugh, cry, kiss and say goodbye.

1) **Make peace** with it and find the pearl of wisdom buried beneath the wound.

2) **Envision greater**; there is victory in your valley. Start to see your way stronger.

3) **Impact and inspire** someone else with your truth of what is possible when you dare to defy the odds stacked against you.

The past is behind you, and the present is filled with treasures without measure. You are still alive. I dare you to lift your head and thrive. I dare you to dream so big your dreams, have dreams.

C.P.I.L.L. Confidence Prescription for Progress

Crownfirmation: I will no longer rehearse the hurt but will celebrate the changes that lead me closer to destiny.

Pause to Ponder: What pain from your past have you harbored in your heart that needs to be tossed far from the shores of your mind?

I Celebrate:

Leadership Lesson Learned:

Lifestyle Elevation: Every Day I Will,

Day 61

Investment

Something deposited with the expectation of receiving a future profit or reward.

Dear Queen,

We often seek for others to invest in our potential before we sacrifice for our success. There are no limits to what you can achieve when you believe. There will be days when you feel completely out of balance. It may feel as if a rushing wind came out of nowhere and knocked you off your feet. You deserve the lifetime investment towards your expansive growth and advancement.

The time it takes to produce tangible rewards will seem long but do not allow the process to irritate and disqualify you from the race. I was inspired by an online influencer when I heard her say that she purchases her online courses before she expects the public to invest in her product. **If you don't believe you're worth the investment, how do you think that will impact your interactions with others?**

A man who sees a well-groomed woman in comparison to a visibly neglected woman will make two different assumptions. One may be perceived to have greater value than the other as a result of time investment in physical aesthetics.

It has been said that price is what you pay, and value is what you get.

The price you pay to be great will transform you into a person with high value. What does that translate into for you? Promotions, all-expense paid trips, inclusion to undisclosed opportunities, access to elite networks and phenomenal perks for doing the secret work. Success is attractive, and winners gravitate towards winners.

If you have yet to see your investment return actualized, keep your eyes gazing into the skies, and listen to the small voice inside saying, *Everything is going to be alright.* You will get through this. You are stronger than you realize. This test is just a reminder of the power you possess. With a long deep breath, pick yourself back up with a renewed focus to best your best self.

Tomorrow we fight harder and roar louder. Don't you dare devalue a single investment of blood, sweat, time, and tears. You've earned your stripes, and victory looks good on you.

C.P.I.L.L. Confidence Prescription for Progress

Crownfirmation: I am profitable. I attract investors everywhere I go, and I am confident in my choices.

Pause to Ponder: Whose potential would you like to invest in and what successful leader would you desire to sharpen your cognitive faculties?

I Celebrate:

Leadership Lesson Learned:

Lifestyle Elevation: Every Day I Will,

Day 62

Start

To begin a course, journey, activity or undertaking. To give attention to something. To bring into being.

Dear Queen,

Have you ever found yourself sitting on the doorsteps of destiny wondering what direction your feet should move toward? There are many paths that lead to your next destination of greatness yet because there are countless options, we often find ourselves stuck in a rut of indecision. **The power rests in your ability to make a swift decision and detach from the outcome.** Detach from the fear of failure. Detach from the opinion of others. Detach from the disappointments. Detach from the unknown and embrace the beauty that rests in the present moment.

Those who procrastinate are waiting for someone to 'save' them and do all the work. They want the result, but have zero interest in doing the work to get there. The call to entrepreneurship was always ringing in my ear, and I answered it years ago after attending a workshop entitled the Spirit of Entrepreneurship. The woman teaching it was my first up close and personal example of an African American female business owner. Later she would become my trusted advisor, partner, and beloved friend. At that crossroad, I desired a role model, someone leading by example was inspiration enough for me to launch into the mysterious world of entrepreneurship.

I have had innumerable conversations with entrepreneurs, and one statement that frequently arises is, "I don't know where to start." We must be aware of the underlying subtlety of self-sabotage. It wears many masks and if you are not discerning it can easily rob you of seeing your potential actualized.

One of my favorite quotes for taking action when all the pieces have yet to appear is by Theodore Roosevelt. **"Do what you can, with what you have, right where you are."** You have limitless resources at your fingertips if you would dare to look outside of your current problems. There is always a solution readily available if you are open to discovery.

We can easily find ourselves overwhelmed with a tsunami of unproductive thoughts? If you serve in any leadership capacity, this mind storm can attack you unexpectedly at a moment's notice. There will be times that there is so much to do, you don't know what to do. During high-pressure seasons in your work and home life, it is important to recognize internal stressors. It is vital that one deciphers what tasks require pertinent attention and others that are merely time wasters.

How do we create new momentum when the wind in our sails has whisked away from us? I believe the main key is found in the brilliance of Johann Wolfgang von Goethe who stated, "What you can do or dream you can do-begin it. Boldness has genius, power, and magic in it. Only engage, and the mind grows heated. Begin it, and the work will be completed."

Here are the steps you'll need to take to move from mundane to magnificent:

1) **Begin again**. Start the article. Pick up the phone and book the appointment. Motion begets motion.

2) **Follow-up**. Give yourself a timeline for obtaining results to the effort invested and seeds planted for a successful harvest.

3) **Finish what you've started**. Loose ends must be clipped. Every time you complete an assignment your confidence level will skyrocket.

There is magnificent power in beginning and finishing your predetermined goals. Our days are filled with priceless and sometimes painstaking moments. I encourage you to convert your moments into momentum by seeking to produce a continual pattern of optimal and tangible results in every endeavor.

As I look in retrospect, most of my achievements were preceded by adversity. I learned to dig deep in the cavern of my soul for precious pearls of inspiration to move forward despite the odds stacked against me. I was not an honor roll student. In fact, I was the opposite of the class president and valedictorian.

Today, my life is completely different. Every day is filled with new and delightful surprises. I speak across the nation, write on authority-based platforms, host my own radio show, empower women through coaching, image consulting and inspirational products, etc. It all started with saying yes to success and nothing less. Did I have extremely difficult days where I wanted to throw in the towel? Absolutely. If I gave up on my dreams, there would be innumerable lives who would never experience the gift of hope that I was destined to share with those in despair. I've designed a vision bigger and brighter than the darkest nights that seek to haunt my goals.

If you are waiting for the proverbial someday or one day, today is that day.

C.P.I.L.L. Confidence Prescription for Progress

Crownfirmation: I am resplendent. I am regal. I am resilient. I am the roar that fear has been waiting for.

Pause to Ponder: Write about an event or accomplishment where you demonstrated the courage to start. What wisdom did you gain about yourself, life and others?

I Celebrate:

Leadership Lesson Learned:

Lifestyle Elevation: Every Day I Will,

Day 63

Priceless

Having a value beyond any price.

Dear Queen,

Many women are working themselves to death because they've lost sight of their pricelessness. The definition of priceless means, so precious that it's value cannot be determined or calculated, costly because of rarity and quality, unique and irreplaceable, having value beyond any price and more valuable than any amount of money can buy.

Step outside of your shell and unveil your true self. Open your spiritual eyes and witness the divine beauty that resides deep down inside. Your life is a rose petal, delicate and fragile. Why do you choose to hide from your own sacred light? Take two steps forward and breathe again, love again, rise again, believe again, trust again, hope again, feel again, dream again, live again, expect again and reach again. Leap outside of your mind and shine brightly. You've traveled too far to forget who you are. Your Majesty, you have an important date with destiny. The definition of worthy is qualified for admiration, respect, and recognition.

"You need to fall in love with who you are right now, flaws and all, before you can love a better version of yourself."

–Keri of Columbia, S.C.

Your significance is more substantive than the number on a scale and more astounding than counting calories. It is the liberty to fully accept and showcase your real self.

Take a deep breath for a moment and center within. Quietly listen to the rhythm of your soul's desires. You are the crown, esteemed and highly valuable.

A keen awareness of your innate worth will give you a cutting-edge advantage on any stage in the world. The invisible crown of confidence will often be the determining factor between a win and a loss. Intently ascend into what's next, fiercely, authentically and relentlessly loving thyself.

In order to get to the core of feeling that you have no value, determine the point of entry and uproot the fallacy. I remember when I was learning to ride a bicycle and scarring my knees when I would fall. My dad said, "You cannot be a model if you have scars." Those words shaped my impressionable mind. One day, I chose to live free from the unrealistic expectations and standards of others. I had to tell myself, "I am not pretty like the women on the cover of magazines. I am pretty like me." There are millions who will never show their face because of the fear of judgment from others. I am on a mission to change that. Imperfection is your superpower!

"It's time to show yourself off. You've got what it takes to step out of the shadows and claim your spotlight. Accepting your value means understanding beauty means more than fitting into someone else's cookie cutter mold. It's realizing what a miracle your body really is—what it can survive and what it can do. It's just deciding not to miss out on all the joy that's possible in your world. Whatever it is for you, embrace it.

"Too many of us have permitted ourselves to be sidelined in the game of life because of features we saw as flaws. I'm too short. I'm too flabby. I'm physically challenged. I'm getting wrinkles. Maybe someone commented unkindly to your "imperfection" and to ward off future judgments you feared you'd get for being less than perfect, your authentic-self started disappearing.

"If people can't see you, they can't find you lacking. Until the day you decide to be invincible and no longer invisible."

–Weight Watchers

During a re-branding photo shoot, my photographer told me to close my eyes and open again to refresh them. That is exactly what we must do after we've experienced disappointments that leave us disenchanted. Close your eyes, and when you open them, see yourself through a fresh set of lens, living in a garden of joy, walking down the red carpet of beauty and ascending a skyscraper to greatness.

Your value is priceless with or without a significant other. Be internally resolved that you are worthy of the best life has to offer, you are worthy of honor, you are worthy of happiness, you are worthy of the finer things in life, you are worthy of peace, you are worthy of success, you are worthy of abundance, you are worthy of prosperity, you are worthy of good health, you are worthy of wholeness, you are worthy of everything you dare to dream.

C.P.I.L.L. Confidence Prescription for Progress

Crownfirmation: My self-worth is not defined by disappointments; it is determined by my internal belief and verbal declaration.

Pause to Ponder: What negative experience left you feeling devalued and how can you re-define your worth?

I Celebrate:

Leadership Lesson Learned:

Lifestyle Elevation: Every Day I Will,

Day 64

Emerge

To manifest or rise from an obscure or inferior position or condition or unknown place.

Dear Queen,

It was in the depths of hardship and where I realized I could no longer be a spectator in the game of life. It became instantly paramount to begin participating at a higher resolve if I desired to do more than survive merely to stay alive. In creating our own wealth, we must continually rise above adversity and learn how to successfully thrive.

Some women are destroyed by the fire, and others are built by its flames. You deserve the finer things in life. The beauty that you will behold is worth every ache you've had to endure in your soul. Can you envision, remarkable destinations, global sophistication, iconic travel, bodacious beliefs taking you to a palace of prominence and the world at your feet?

In a state of emergency, dare to emerge and see the life of your dreams. You've outgrown the background and the comfort zone. Now is the time to graciously accept your assigned seat at the forefront of victory.

One of the most inspiring stories of rising above the ashes I have found was about Michele Hoskins. Her determination to pursue her vision despite divorce, low income, and major health issues was astounding. She decided to create a new product from her great grandmother's syrup recipe. After she had the syrup formulated and packaged, she took the products to local grocery stores, asking them to stock the product and if they sold, she would invoice them. This worked well, but she had bigger ideas. Her goal was to get the syrup into Denny's restaurants.

She got in touch with the right people at Denny's, and they told her no. But that did not stop her. She made it a habit of calling them every single Monday at 10:30 a.m. for two years.

When Denny's hired a new CEO, they told him about this woman who called every Monday at 10:30. "What does she want?" the CEO asked. "She wants us to use her product," they replied.

This was during the time that Denny's was suffering from a blow to their reputation after being sued for treating African American's poorly in their restaurant in past years. Michelle Hoskins happened to be African American. The CEO was baffled that these people had turned her down for so long, this is exactly the kind of business partnership they needed.

Not long after, Michelle had the contract with Denny's, and now she is a multi-millionaire.

We often convince ourselves that no-one would be interested in what we have to offer, that someone else is doing what we desire to do. We believe we don't have the credentials, we aren't pretty enough, we don't have the income, or we don't have the guru of the hour. It's just a defense mechanism to keep us playing small. You were created to live large and in charge. Find out who you have yet to become. Most people stop at the start—but not you. Make the quantum leaps and focus on evolving every day. Step by step. Laser in on what matters most to you.

"Be daring, be different, be impractical, be anything that will assert integrity of purpose and imaginative vision against the play-it-safers, the creatures of the commonplace and slaves of the ordinary."

–Cecil Beaton

You have what it takes, but it will take everything you've got. You were not built to break down; you were designed to breakthrough. Against all the odds, bet on yourself. Stack the odds in your favor and surprise yourself with what you can do.

C.P.I.L.L. Confidence Prescription for Progress

Crownfirmation: I will emerge energized and infused with an unwavering focus. The strength I need dwells inside of me.

Pause to Ponder: What radical act are you willing to demonstrate in the face of pain to emerge again unscathed?

I Celebrate:

Leadership Lesson Learned:

Lifestyle Elevation: Every Day I Will,

Magnificence

Impressive beauty or greatness.

Dear Queen,

If magnificence is the robe of royalty, then confidence is the crown of authority. There is a cutting-edge advantage that will allow you to stand out in any crowd. The invisible crown of internal confidence will often be the determining factor between a win and a loss. Many individuals forfeit countless achievements due to being unaware of the top five thieves of magnificence.

1) **Comparison.** In the school of business, we are taught to study our competition. In the royal academy of excellence, a true queen understands that she is unique by design which is her competitive advantage. It is paramount that you study every aspect of your being. This includes being honest with your strengths and weaknesses. The question to focus on is, "Are you the best that you can be?" The amount of effort that you will be investing in the cultivation of personal greatness leaves no room for comparison to others.

2) **Past failures.** It takes an unflinching audacity to rise from the pit of past disappointments with a renewed vigor to reach new heights. Winston Churchill expressly stated, "Success is not

final, failure is not fatal: it is the courage to continue that counts." In the heart of a crown bearer, there is no space for housing debilitating thoughts of yesterday. Become preoccupied with winning until you possess victory.

3) **Lack of preparation**. It has been said, "Victory loves preparation." Every day presents an opportunity to prepare for the next win. To create a lifestyle of winning it requires a champion state of mind. Are you willing to go the extra mile? Are you willing to become extremely uncomfortable? Are you willing to rise early and go to bed late if that's what it takes? Are you willing to do what others won't until you can do what others can't? This is your life. How will you live it?

4) **Fear**. Recently, I saw a homeless man in the parking lot of Walmart holding a sign that said, 'don't judge me'. This is one of the number one fears that hold most individuals back from chasing their passion. The opinion of others has no power unless you yield to their words. The world is full of critics who stand on the sidelines of life haunted by their own fears, attempting to stop dreamers dead in their tracks. Your beliefs must be more powerful than any anxiety, terror or dread.

5) **Negativity**. How do you combat negativity when it seems to continually assail you on a daily basis from countless media platforms? I believe Emily Dickinson said it best. "I dwell in possibilities." There is no other place I would rather be. This requires intentionality and constant watchfulness to every thought that comes across your mind. Our beliefs are potent

seeds that create full-grown trees in our mind producing ripe or rotten fruit. Be diligent in weeding out every negative thought; your future depends on it.

Lastly, before you step foot on any stage remember that you are the crown, esteemed, and highly valuable. Be aware of ego, because it is a death sentence to magnificence. I will never arrive until I die. How long will you continue to pretend that you were born to be average?

Embrace your divine essence. Love yourself fiercely and relentlessly.

"The opportunity of a lifetime must be seized within the lifetime of the opportunity."

–Leonard Ravenhill

C.P.I.L.L. Confidence Prescription for Progress

Crownfirmation: I was not fashioned to be popular, but tailor-made to be potent.

Pause to Ponder: What person, place or thing have you allowed to strip you of your magnificence, power or beauty?

I Celebrate:

Leadership Lesson Learned:

Lifestyle Elevation: Every Day I Will,

Day 66

Sacred

Highly valued and important.

Dear Queen,

Higher dimensions require heightened discipline. Average will always be on the outside looking in. It's up to you to remain one thousand steps ahead. Who you once were does not serve who you are or who you shall be. Ashes to ashes, dust to dust; the past is over. Focusing on the future is a must. Leaders lead and followers follow.

In order to honor the sacred, it is vital to slow down long enough to express thankfulness on a daily basis. I am no stranger to adversity from childhood to present. I believe the key to abundance and a hopeful perspective amidst challenging times is to treasure the entire journey.

There are countless benefits associated with gratitude ranging from enhanced sleep, improved relationships along with better psychological and physical health. If you desire to become more grateful, you must begin with acknowledging your desire to change. Once you are aware of the need to create a new norm, ask yourself, are you ready to make the commitment daily until it becomes second nature? There will be temptations to revert to old mental paradigms. Who have you invited to support this change and hold you accountable? Additionally, create a list of seven powerful reasons that this change is important to you.

Here are three simple ways to cultivate a spirit of gratefulness and honor the sacred every day:

1) **Purchase a gratitude journal.** It is easy to lose sight of the many blessings you have in your life when you choose not to reflect in a quiet space to give thanks. I love to create what I call, grains of gratitude based on the current calendar month. If it's November, I would start the day with eleven grains of appreciation and before bed journal eleven grains of appreciation for things I encountered throughout my day.

2) **One a day.** Think about the special people that are close to your heart, especially if you are married. In order to avoid taking our family and friends for granted, verbally express one thing to them that you are thankful for. I always say, "It's the little things that make a big difference." What you appreciate, appreciates.

3) **Serve the less fortunate.** This is one act that keeps my heart continuously in a humble posture. Whenever I interact or see the homeless, I immediately consider the richness of my life. I begin to give thanks for a roof over my head, shoes on my back and food on the table. One day I witnessed an older man bathing on the street, and I realized I took something as simple as the ability to shower in private for granted.

The more grateful you are, the more attractive you will be to others.

Honestly, how many people do you know long to be in the presence of complainers? Everyone is fighting their own private battles; you can choose to be the wind beneath their wings or the rain on their parade.

"Gratitude turns what we have into enough, and more. It turns denial into acceptance, chaos into order, confusion into clarity. It makes sense of our past, brings peace for today, and creates a vision for tomorrow."

–Melody Beattie

Let's put into practice what we have learned and affirm the power of gratitude:

I feel an abundance of gratitude for everything I have and receive every day.

I clearly see the beauty of life that flourishes around me.

I am so grateful for every person and everything in my life.

My needs and desires are generously met. For this I am thankful.

At the end of each day, I take a moment to reflect and be grateful.

C.P.I.L.L. Confidence Prescription for Progress

Crownfirmation: In the heights of the battlefield, I will not bow my sword in retreat or defeat. These are the days of roar, and with all my might I'm pressing forward. I choose faith over fear. I choose focus over frustration. I choose calm over chaos. I choose wellness over worry. I choose positivity over pessimism. I choose liberty over limitations. Every moment of every hour—come hell or high water—I choose to stand in prevailing power as the sun blazing through the clouds.

Pause to Ponder: What mindful practices will you incorporate in each day to create space to honor and cultivate the sacred?

I Celebrate:

Leadership Lesson Learned:

Lifestyle Elevation: Every Day I Will,

Arise

To come up or out of something into existence. Implies rapid or sudden emerging to move upward.

Dear Queen,

Who you are today represents a glimpse of the greatness that is waiting to be showcased. If you were to take inventory of your entire life what message does it speak? Are you aware of the incredible power you possess? The intellectual prowess embedded in your cerebral cortex, to you it appears simple and to others seemingly complex.

How do you walk in your power when you simultaneously feel imprisoned by your pain? The first key is to remember you possess a divine purpose on earth that only you can fulfill. The world needs you to survive, to thrive and to arise.

You are stronger than your struggle. You house a heart of faith and fortitude designed to withstand the most vehement storms. The journey is laden with twists and turns, vision and valleys, magnificence and mayhem, dreams and disappointments. After the relentless raindrops never forget to search for the radiant rainbows hidden in your soul.

After you've experienced constant turmoil and one battle wound after another, it is easy to lose sight of why you are still in the fight. This is when it becomes paramount to rediscover your flaming desires like the phoenix and rebirth the queen of comeback who is fueled by fire. Passion must remain a faithful guide. You cannot bulldoze through mental barriers if passivity is behind the wheel of your destiny.

The path to your eternal ending demands a spirit of perseverance especially when life is not all pies in the sky. The question remains, can you forge forward in the face of tumultuous troubles barraging in the night? One minuscule act has the power to create a massive impact. Don't lose momentum. Keep moving one foot in front of the other, day by day.

Finally, you owe it to yourself to pick your crown up from off the ground, walk with your head held high, bold and proud. You are not a mistake, but a precious miracle.

"If these were her last moments, then at least she would go down fighting, to the sound of exquisite music.

It was time.

One breath—another.

She was the heir of fire.

She was fire, and light, and ash, and embers. She was Aelin Fireheart, and she bowed to no-one and nothing, save the crown that was hers by blood and survival and triumph."

–Sarah J. Maas

C.P.I.L.L. Confidence Prescription for Progress

Crownfirmation: I am a promise, driven by purpose, fueled by passion and willing to persevere until my destiny is fulfilled.

Pause to Ponder: What words of encouragement do you need to hear from yourself to rise in prevailing power?

I Celebrate:

Leadership Lesson Learned:

Lifestyle Elevation: Every Day I Will,

Shift

To change the place, position, or direction of something or someone to change how something is done or how people think about something.

Dear Queen,

Are you aware of the power embedded deeply in your subconscious? I once read a quote by Heather Dominick who stated, "A shift in perception leads to a shift in action. A shift in action leads to a shift in results." As one who specializes in mindset mastery, I can immediately identify the mental and emotional state of the individual I am speaking with. **One of the greatest gifts we have been given as women is intuition.** I believe we instinctively know when it is time to re-design our lives. A primary indicator is a loss of joy and peace, when life seems more of a chore than a celebration. Another hint is when you are no longer challenged to grow. Underdeveloped potential will leave you feeling frustrated and dissatisfied. You will know it's time when you can no longer settle for less than what you believe you are worth.

When I am ready for an internal overhaul and mindset elevation, I instantly create a vision board of what I want. The seventeen vision boards on my office wall are placed up high so I can see them every day. Visualization is a proven formula to manifesting your deepest desires. What you think about you bring about.

Once you see what you want and boldly say it out loud, you must be prepared to courageously seize it.

In between seeing and saying is where internal opposition arises to prevent you from possessing. This is why it is critical to remove yourself from toxic individuals and environments where you are not free to thrive.

Three forms of mental blocks that will prevent you from moving forward:

1) **Resistance.** Defined as fighting against change. You know what needs to be done, but you are unwilling to do the work necessary to shift your life.

2) **Avoidance.** Defined as withdrawing from something. This is very common in women as we tend to allow our emotions to dictate our behavior. What does this look like? Hiding under the covers or like the ostrich burying your head in the sand. You cannot conquer what you refuse to confront.

3) **Dissonance.** Defined as lack of harmony or agreement, inconsistency between the beliefs one holds or between one's actions and one's beliefs. How this shows up is when you say you want to write a book, but you don't believe you are smart enough to accomplish this goal.

What are you willing to change today that will impact tomorrow? It takes heart to start now, to start over, and to start something beautiful. Let it begin with you.

C.P.I.L.L. Confidence Prescription for Progress

Crownfirmation: I will shift from my mind from lack to luxury, from worry to worthiness, from pain to promise and from fear to focus.

Pause to Ponder: What small shifts will you make to perform at an optimal state of being?

I Celebrate:

Leadership Lesson Learned:

Lifestyle Elevation: Every Day I Will,

Finish

To come to the end of a course, task, or undertaking which conveys a strong sense of finality. The result of a finishing processor the last part of something.

Dear Queen,

The ability to achieve lofty goals start with a desire to win. Yet, more will be required. You must become determined to win. In order to ascend even higher, it is paramount that you become dedicated to winning to avoid falling into the abyss of losing.

There are Olympic athletes who train for years to compete in a one-hundred-meter race that takes less than ten seconds to complete. We're talking cheetah speed. They must possess strength, power, and flexibility. We each have our own individual race to run.

Are you mentally prepared to persevere to the finish line? Expect the unexpected. Get ready to run in the rain, run through the pain, run when you're feeling faint, run on the brink, run in the chaos, run after major loss, run in the face of danger, run with a heart full of anger, run through frustration, run after devastation, run through the mistakes, run in the face of hate, run in the middle of the night, and if you are going to run, make sure you run for your life.

Tony Robbins said, "Passion is the genesis of genius."

If you desire the type of success that is lasting, it is imperative that you strengthen your internal stance especially in seasons of struggle. The definition of stance is a person's posture, a mental or emotional position, a rationalized intellectual attitude or the position assumed by an athlete preparing for action.

How often have you allowed the start to stop you? Cultivating a track record of success requires an ability to follow through until completion. **Are you going to be known as the person who can make it happen or the one who leaves her work undone with everyone asking where has she gone?**

Stop ghosting your greatness. In the words of Henry Ford, "You can't build a reputation on what you are going to do." It's time to create a monumental shift in your inner strength. You must develop a 'you can't stop me' mentality as you turn your dreams into reality.

C.P.I.L.L. Confidence Prescription for Progress

Crownfirmation: I will complete every task from start to finish. I refuse to quit until I win.

Pause to Ponder: What project, goal or task have you placed on the back burner of procrastination that needs to be completed today?

I Celebrate:

Leadership Lesson Learned:

Lifestyle Elevation: Every Day I Will,

Reign

Royal authority to rule as a king, queen or, emperor. To be the best or the most powerful A quality existing to such a degree in a place or situation that it affects everything about that place or situation.

Dear Queen,

Can you imagine how impactful a leader you could become if you were committed to a lifestyle of reigning? If you desire to create an entirely different outcome, it is essential to remember that change is a choice. We often have an extra boost of motivation at the bourgeoning heights of a new season. You have created a new set of skills to persevere in unfavorable weather. That is how you reign, one crowning thought at a time.

Over the course of seventy days, we've identified negative habitual patterns that are preventing you from embarking on an extraordinary path towards greatness. We've confronted deep and dark pain that has held you in captivity. The power you possess is eternal, the strength you inhabit cannot be stripped away, and the beauty you radiate cannot be diminished.

Make being the best at who you are and all you set out to do your constant aim. The truth will be your shield in the fiery furnace of affliction. The audacity to live powerfully will create substantial opportunities to be greeted by prosperity. On the days that you doubt your divine birthright, think of Esther, a Jewish orphan who was selected by a Persian king to be queen out of a sea of beautiful women. The Persian meaning of Esther is star, and her Jewish name meant myrtle tree. That is the magnificence of transformation; it will turn a bland tree into a beaming star. You were created to sparkle and shine. **Never allow anything or anyone to dim your light.**

You are worthy of the best life has to offer. You are stronger than any struggle. You are bold, beautiful and brilliant. You are resilient, radiant and relentless. You are one of a kind by design and not default. You are healed, whole, and worthy of unconditional love. You are full of potential and limitless possibilities. You are tenacious and triumphant in the face of adversity. You are walking in a peace that surpasses understanding. You are standing tall as a tower. This your moment and your hour. You are crowned with prevailing power.

Be happy and pleased

with the woman you see standing

audaciously authentic

on the cusp of prophetic destiny.

Your radiant light is a true reflection of God's love,

intersecting with heaven and earth.

Be happy and pleased with

the way you continue to conquer mountains of adversity.

Your strength in the valley of challenge

is a testament to God's faithfulness to draw near,

after hearing your faintest whisper in His ear.

Delighted is the woman whose God is the Lord.

On today, be of good cheer and

choose His shielding presence, over the shadows of fear.

May you experience the life you've always imagined. May you walk into new dimensions of power, authority, and influence. May you be open to give grace and receive boundless love from others. May you embrace all that is pure and release anything that is toxic to your well-being. May you find a resting place in the garden of truth and refuse to sleep in a bed of lies. May you gain clarity and insight surrounding the next steps to take towards your divine destiny. **May your leading example be worthy of imitation of the days of your life.**

Today, ask yourself one question: What can I change in my daily routine to perform at optimal levels? What was your greatest self-discovery aha moment on this seventy-day journey of developing your inner queenfidence? Share it with us on Facebook @queenfidenceimage or Instagram @queenfidenceimageconsulting

Go and be you in an extraordinary way. Go and see something you've never had the courage to see. Go and spread hope to forgotten souls who desire unconditional love. Go and live free from the shackles of an unpleasant history.

Go and run wild in your imagination and explore limitless possibilities. Go and reign now, powerfully in your divine destiny. It's time to shift from looking in the mirror to walking in the manifestation.

C.P.I.L.L. Confidence Prescription for Progress

Crownfirmation: I will do what queens do, I will rise, rule and reign. Let it reign in my finances. Let it reign in my business. Let it reign, in my spirit. Let it reign in my home. Let it reign in every transaction. Let it reign in every plan. Let it reign in every relationship. Let it reign wherever I travel. Let it reign in my vision. Let it reign in my health. Let it reign, in my mind. Let it reign as I walk. Let it reign when I talk. Let it reign before day breaks. Let it reign as the sun sets. Let it reign bountifully. Let it reign supernaturally. Let it reign exponentially.

I Celebrate:

Leadership Lesson Learned:

Lifestyle Elevation: Every Day I Will,

Queenfidence Global Image Consulting is designed for 21st-century peak performing executives. We are advocates of wholistic womanhood. We value wellness over workaholism, serenity over sacrifice, calmness over chaos and health over hustle. We believe in longevity, vitality and reciprocity. The five pillars of power that energize our internal being are affirmation, awareness, appreciation, acknowledgement and action.

The rewards of our personal time investment are emotional stability, spiritual strength, mental sharpness, physical stamina and financial success. We choose to honor the sacred beauty of self-care in order to preserve our worth and wellness. We believe our feminine nature is to be nurtured above all and not severely neglected at any cost.

We aim to empower emerging, established and enterprising female leaders through four components of change: mindset mastery, massive momentum, magnetic messaging and potential maximization. Queenfidence is a powerful state of living and an eternal way of being.

www.queenfidence.com

"We Train to Reign."

Made in the USA
Columbia, SC
14 March 2020